Personality Marketing:

Join Your Industry's A-List by Embracing Your Inner Nerd

Table of Contents

Chapter Four: How to Make Personality Marketing Work for Your Unique Situation (Even If It Seems Impossible Right Now)   74

Chapter Five: How to Position Yourself as a Game Changer, Even If You Feel Like a Big Fat Imposter Right Now   99

For Sam

who sat patiently in my tummy
while I wrote this book

Nothing great was ever achieved without enthusiasm.

Ralph Waldo Emerson

Chapter One:

How to Become a Major Player In Your Industry

Even If You're Strapped for Time AND Cash,
Even If You're Not a Supermodel
or a Fancy Pants Type,
and Even if You're Not Yet Sure
What Business You're Really In...

Let's Go!

Psssssst...

I've got a mind-blowing idea I want you to wrap your head around right now.

I'll whisper it, so you can really feel how juicy it is, okay? You ready?

*If you listen very closely and apply the stuff I'm about to teach you, you might never have to engage in cold calling, social media stalking or one-to-one prospecting, **EVER again.***

Is that not **the *coolest* thing you've ever heard?**

Heck YES it is!

It's amazing!

Not only that, but if you apply this stuff *well,* you'll be able to attract your dream customers and make more money than you ever thought possible while working WAY less (and having way MORE FUN) than you are now.

The principles and strategies you're about to learn are behind nearly ALL of the biggest "internet famous" success stories you've heard about online.

By the time we're finished here, you're going to know exactly how my peers and I are selling products and services at all different price points-- *yes, even high ticket stuff*, without all of the mind-numbing trappings of old-school sales.

Which, as you might imagine is a dream come true. Because old-school sales strategies are laaaaaame.

What does life look like on the other side of old-school selling?

All of those exhausting, frustrating hours I used to spend prospecting for new leads online and talking to people who were never going to buy?

Gone. *No more prospecting for me.*

HUZZAH!!!

And it's a good thing, too-- as I'm writing this, I'm about to welcome BABY BULLEN #4 into the family, which means-- *ain't NOBODY got time to be chasing leads and selling on the phone!*

These people come to ME now.

Every single day, I've got a fresh batch of new sales notifications in my inbox.

Mind you, these are people I've *never* talked to before, one on one.

When I ask them why they bought, they're telling me things like, *"I've been watching your videos and I just **know** you're the one who can help me. I know you're legit and whatever you're selling, I just knew I **wanted** some!"*

Doesn't that sound *awesome*?

Don't you want your sales process to be like that?

I know! I know you do!

Everybody wants that, right?

So how does it work... and how do we make it work for you?

Well, I'll tell you. But first... I should probably introduce myself.

My name is Brittany Bullen and I'm a nerd.

I geek out about ad strategy, persuasion and storytelling ALL DAY long. Whether I'm working with our agency clients over at NerdyGirl.co, with students in my courses or with coaching clients, there's one big passion that brings it all together:

It is my mission in life to help awesome entrepreneurs like YOU in your noble quests to sell more stuff, serve more people and change more lives than you ever thought possible.

My favorite way to do that is to teach you how to use a very exciting marketing strategy that I like to call "Personality Marketing"-- **the art of thinking like a *media company* first and a *salesperson* second**, using the distinct characteristics of *your personality* to set yourself (or your company) apart from your competitors.

· ·

How to Turn Your Company Into a Media Company and EXPLODE Your Online Presence

All the biggest marketing minds of our generation seem to be using **the "media company" buzzword,** don't they?

They're preaching that we need to treat our companies like media companies FIRST and purveyors of whatever it is we sell SECOND.

But how do we actually DO that?

With Personality Marketing, that's how. And you're about to get an in-depth look at exactly how it works.

SPOILER ALERT:

It's NOT about publishing endless amounts of boring, formulaic content...

It's not about posting pictures of your dinner and expecting that to help you sell stuff...

It's about finding the perfect balance of PERSONALITY ELEMENTS (to make it engaging and emotionally compelling)

and tried-and-true MARKETING PRINCIPLES (to make it effective).

This typically involves a strategic combination of online content (ideally video), paid advertising and marketing automation.

To help my clients apply this "media company concept" effectively, I look at them while wearing two "hats" *(being both a social media advertising consultant and a playwright/performer)*, thinking carefully about how to **draw out certain elements of your and/or your company's story** to position you as an industry leader-- a member of your industry's "A-List", if you will.

We then do whatever we can to weave that positioning and strategic storytelling into your whole marketing funnel (from the ads to the videos to the emails and anything else that might be required in between) so that you **build a powerful relationship of trust** with your ideal customer, **make more money** and **grow your business as rapidly and profitably as possible.**

Confused?

That's okay. Lots of people are.

I'm here to help.

But... I'm getting WAYYYY ahead of myself.

Let's start at the very beginning, shall we?

(If you're humming a song from "The Sound of Music" right now, we should hang out.)

• •

What the CRAP Happened to Social Media Marketing (and What's an Entrepreneur to DO About It?)

Once upon a time, I had the *totally* bucket-list-worthy opportunity to produce and perform in my very own original musical on 42nd street, a stone's throw from Broadway, as part of the New York Musical Theatre Festival.

It. Was. *Incredible.*

It was a dream come true.

But when it was over, it was just... *over...*

...and I was sitting there at home with my boys (who are delightfully low-maintenance, thank heavens) thinking, *now what?*

I was sick of working my royal Rastafarian nay-nays off (pardon the Cool Runnings reference) for *no* pay, so **I set out to make some money**.

I figured I might as well put my writing degree to good use, so I started doing some freelance blogging (until like two seconds later I realized *I hated freelance blogging*)...

But I was having no trouble at all finding clients, so I started contracting the work out to my friends.

That was the beginning of my marketing services company, NerdyGirl.co.

I had this brilliant idea (or so I thought) that selling content marketing services on commission would be **the ultimate home business opportunity** for somebody like me, who was home with kids and wanted to make legit money and use their talents and education without the hassle of building an agency from the ground up.

The vision was simple: I would create the infrastructure and find the talent and handle the marketing and branding stuff, and then our salespeople would earn commissions for any new client business they brought in.

They would also serve as the account manager and continue to manage those client relationships, acting as the liaison between the client and any freelance talent needed to get the job done.

I was filled with a sense of purpose and a duty to make life better for my peers-- because I *knew* how big of a deal it was for my self-esteem to be able to earn money AND have the flexibility to be there for my kids at the same time!

The idea began to catch on almost instantly...

Mostly as a result of my going out and networking and telling our story, we brought in a bunch of great clients within the first couple of months after launching.

But there was a problem.

Early on, the vast majority of our clients hired us to 1) write blog posts for them, and/or 2) curate and share content for them on social media.

I didn't know this at the time, but social media was about to change for us *and* for our clients in a *really* big way...

The fact of the matter, **across almost *every* industry**, is this:

Social media *advertising* has changed the game for business owners, and content saturation has made the problem even *worse*.

Watching the results of our efforts for our clients, this shift became very clear to me very quickly.

That said, it may or may not yet be clear to you, so let me explain myself a bit.

You see, before all of the major social networks introduced paid advertising, **it was *much easier* for business owners to get attention** simply by posting content on a regular basis. That's why back then, it was enough to post generic curated content from popular blogs and the occasional inspiring quote graphic on Facebook and Twitter and call it a day.

A similar problem has appeared for marketers who used to rely heavily on blogging. Before, it was much easier to use search engine optimization to rank your blog posts high enough on Google to bring you plenty of free traffic... but sadly, nowadays, the internet has become **so saturated with content** that THAT strategy gets harder and harder to pull off, too!

So, what's an entrepreneur to do?

Well, I'll tell you what *doesn't work*, because that's something I know *for sure:* **creating average content in average quantities without any paid promotion and expecting to make a profit** from it as soon as *yesterday?* That's what *doesn't work.*

Not any more, at least.

And here's why:

Over the past few years, the amount of content we *consume* on a daily basis has remained relatively consistent, while the amount of content being *produced* has absolutely SKYROCKETED.

What that means for us as marketers is that it's a lot more likely for our content to get ignored, *especially* if it doesn't stand out.

But with this somewhat scary and/or depressing rise in competition, there is also **a VERY EXCITING new world** out there and a TON of opportunity for those who will open the gates and seize the day...

(Cue the music from Newsies...)

• •

Don't Be Afraid and Don't Delay...

Yes. Things *are* competitive out there.

Yes. Advertising online gets more and more expensive as competition increases.

HOWEVER...

We now live in a time when average folks like you and me have access to more power, more influence and more attention *than ever before in history.*

We used to have to be "picked". **Today, we can pick ourselves.**

You don't need a major network's permission to be the star of the show-- *you can create your OWN show!*

And that's exactly what I'm here to help you do.

Today's online content creators are the celebrities of tomorrow, because more and more, media consumers are shifting their attention online.

And where attention goes, influence follows.

So **if you want to make your mark on the world, it has never been easier to do so**-- so long as you can *create content worthy of paying attention to* and build a strategy that will actually *get the right people to pay attention to it!*

Think about it--

Do you follow any "online influencers" now?

Do you watch their videos? Read their emails? Buy their products? Listen to their advice?

Most of us do-- whether we admit it or not.

These self-made a-listers may not be "famous" in the traditional sense, but their content has earned them the right to YOUR precious attention, and *that is NO small thing, my friend!*

Advertisers pay MILLIONS to get their sales message in front of you for 30 seconds during the super bowl, and YOU have the opportunity to show up in someone's inbox and newsfeed EVERY DAY, if you want to, for *mere pennies...* if not for FREE!

*Are you seeing how **incredible** this is yet?*

Mass media has been the world's greatest advertising machine since the invention of the TV set, but *things are changing--* and it's up to YOU to determine whether those changes will **eat your business alive,** or fuel your ability to **create a MASSIVE EXPLOSION of growth** and impact!

(I don't know about you, but that second option sounds quite a bit more appealing...)

Let's figure out how to make this big-time cultural shift work in your favor, shall we?

In order to do that, let's take a look at the writing on the wall and learn a bit from history about how traditional media companies adapted to the first wave of content saturation.

Back in the early days of mass media, there were only a small handful of channels to choose from. Just a handful of options at any given time for the shows we would watch on TV.

And **EVERYBODY watched them.**

Little by little, we saw more shows and more networks and more viewing options being added, until ultimately we ended up with more TV content than we could possibly consume in a lifetime.

Three big shifts happened as a result of content saturation on TV that are worth thinking about today.

Big Shift #1: Goliath Beats David... Most of the Time

First, **the big companies with the deepest pockets dominated** *and will continue to dominate* the media/ entertainment landscape, simply because with money comes greater opportunity to get your stuff out there in front of more people.

This was true in the early days of TV just like it's true on social media now.

As more and more people come to compete, **it gets harder and harder to get your content seen**, *no matter how good it might be.* Even those who are willing to pay for ads are having more and more trouble competing as supply and demand pushes ad costs higher and higher.

The more you can (or are willing to) spend on your ads, the more quickly and easily your "world domination plan" can unfold.

Of course, that all hinges upon how effective your ad strategy is, but we'll get to that soon enough...

Big Shift #2: David Gets Smarter and Seeks Out Hidden Opportunities

During the first wave of content saturation, the smaller TV networks that survived did so by branching out to specialize in content for smaller niche audiences. They set out to create a "cult following" or a **really passionate, really specific fan base** around their shows.

They created those "cult followings" by carefully seeking under-served groups of viewers and creating shows worth "geeking out about" and sharing with like-minded friends and acquaintances.

That's happening online right now, too.

Smart marketers are **narrowing the focus of their content and/or their audience** because they know that's probably going to be their best chance at competing with the "big guys"-- especially if they can create great content for a really *enthusiastic and hungry* audience, which of course is the holy grail.

Big Shift #3: David Beats Goliath (Sometimes, at Least) by Building the Ultimate Weapon

Finally, as more and more entertainment options flooded the television landscape, TV show concepts got **bigger, bolder and more entertaining**. TV producers knew then what internet marketers are only just now beginning to understand-- that *if our content doesn't get better, **we're not going to stay competitive.***

In other words, "me too" ads and cookie-cutter content inspired by tired old courses and automated programs will NOT be sufficient if you want to compete with the major players in your industry.

They can outspend you, and they will.

Unless...

You build a better weapon to compete with.
Or... on second thought, let's drop the "weapon" thing.

I was partying with the David and Goliath metaphor for a second, but I don't want to compare your content to a weapon. It's not a weapon.

We're not out to clobber anyone with our marketing, I hope.

Right? Good.

Let's jump to a friendly fishing metaphor instead.

You know, like, a catch and release type fishing metaphor, where everybody lives happily ever after and no tiny fishies need be harmed.

In order to catch a lot of fish, **what you really need is *better bait***.

Those early experiences with clients at NerdyGirl taught me that mere "content for content's sake" very rarely does the job you want it to do.

If you really want to compete in *today's* marketing landscape, **your content must have that special something extra...**

"What exactly IS the something extra my content needs", you ask?

Your content, to get the best possible results, should be *more* than helpful.

It should be *more* than mildly interesting.

It needs to *create believers*.

• •

How to "Create Believers" (and Why You Need Them)

Why is it so effective to harness the power of your awesome personality in your marketing?

Because when it comes to selling stuff, *belief is everything*.

If I truly believe, for example, that being coached by Tony Robbins will make my life a million times better, *then it probably will,* and I should have no qualms about paying him a million dollars a year for that coaching.

If I don't believe it, I won't pay it.

Tony Robbins knows this, so he also knows that his full time job is not to *sell...* it's to create *believers.*

That's your job now, too.

Never forget-- we determine what we're going to get out of the products and services we buy.

So much of what we do in life gets done simply because **we naturally want to prove our assumptions right.**

If right now you're reading this book and thinking it's a big sack of nonsense and a waste of your time?

You're probably right! It probably is!

For you, anyway.

It *will* be a waste of your time because you've already made that assumption, and thus will spend the rest of your reading time **looking for further proof** to support your assumption..

If, on the other hand, you have a sneaking suspicion that what you're learning here will help you get to that next five, six, seven or even eight figures in your business, then you know what?

It probably will.

And you'll probably want to hear and buy even more from me when we're done here.

That's why as I wrote this book, I knew that my #1 job was further establish the *trust* and *rapport* you feel in our relationship, even (and especially) in the likely event that we've never actually met face to face.

I take that job very seriously because I know that when we buy things, we don't actually buy the *things* themselves...

We buy the way those things make us *feel.*

On more than one occasion I've invested large amounts of money hiring coaches **just because** of the way I feel when I'm around them...

...because to me, *spending money to gain proximity to people who make me feel inspired, confident and powerful is worth every penny.*

If your marketing pushes straight to the sale without creating a relationship with your customer, *just think* of what you might be missing out on!

The power is in the relationship. The experience. The trust. The *belief* in who you are and what you stand for.

Your content, for maximum persuasive power, should lay the foundations of a *meaningful relationship* between you and those who consume it.

We want them to like you.

We want them to trust you.

We want them to BUY from you.

And once they do, we want to keep them coming back for more.

That's the dream, right?

Let's make it happen.

We've already established the harsh reality that social media and the internet in general are NOT what they used to be...

...while it used to be somewhat easy to build a following online without spending a dime, *that's just no longer the case.*

We're so inundated with content, **we're barely even getting through the stuff we've *paid* to learn or consume!**

That makes our jobs as marketers all the more challenging.

You can't expect your content to get randomly discovered and grow an engaged and profitable following. It happens on some rare occasions, but **you certainly can't count on it.**

The way to adapt your online marketing strategy if you want to survive this shift is to become a "professional friend maker" of sorts-- either by using social media as a tool for starting conversations and building relationships one by one *(which is lovely, but NOT the thing we're here to chat about in this book)*, AND/OR creating content that's engaging and compelling enough to lay the foundations of that relationship for you *(which IS what we're going to talk about here).*

That said, it won't be enough to just *create* that content-- you must then strategically *distribute* that content, *to the right audience, repeatedly* in order to **stay relevant, avoid being forgotten and maximize the lifetime value** of your customers.

Chew On THIS

We cannot afford to assume that the prospect will "stay with us" long enough to build a foundation of rapport and trust. We have to make it impossible for the prospect to forget us.

Previously, this was where online marketers relied VERY heavily on email, but today's reality is that **most people's inboxes are so full** that it becomes more and more difficult to rely on that as a primary means of getting in front of *(and staying relevant to)* our respective audiences.

There are quite a few ways we can address that issue. Here are a few:

- We can use chat bots
- We can create groups on a variety of social networks

- We can use direct mail, and...
- We can implement advanced retargeting campaigns to force our message in front of our existing audiences (*in the friendliest of ways, of course*).

But putting the tactical details aside, the reason that personality marketing is needed now more than ever is because *in order for your ideal customer to believe that you really can get them where they want to go,* **they must first EXPERIENCE what it's like to work with you.**

Most "by the book" marketing does not supply that sort of experience-- it's so focused on urgency, conversion optimization and slick sales tactics that the SOUL gets SUCKED right out of it!

No bueno.

Personality marketing is about putting the heart and soul BACK into your message-- combining *the immense persuasive power of real human stories* (conveyed with **sincere human emotion**) with the *immense persuasive power of proven marketing principles* to create a killer (maybe even unbeatable!) combination.

Let me say it another way:

If your marketing has yielded disappointing results for you thus far, it might be because your prospect never got the chance to experience what it really FEELS like to benefit from what you have to offer.

That's why the goal with personality marketing is to employ the very best of your enthusiasm, energy and compassion in order to create the **essential emotional experience** that needs to take place on the road to a purchase decision (*and of course, the bigger the commitment/investment is on the part of the buyer, the more powerful that emotional experience needs to be)!*

But the question then becomes, *what emotions does your prospect need to experience* in order to buy whatever it is you sell?

Let's explore that, shall we?

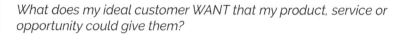

Do This NOW

Write down your answers to the following questions:

What does my ideal customer WANT that my product, service or opportunity could give them?

What EMOTIONAL EXPERIENCE would this person need to have with me in order to believe that I really could help them get the thing they want? How would my marketing need to make them feel?

What does my ideal customer FEAR that my product, service or opportunity could help them avoid?

What EMOTIONAL EXPERIENCE would this person need to have with me in order to believe that I really could help them avoid the thing they fear? How would my marketing need to make them feel?

Now at this point, you're probably thinking,

"Yeah... this is a lovely thing to think through... but NOW what?"

"How do I actually go about CREATING this sort of emotional experience?"

Not to worry. We're going to talk about that in just a minute.

But first, I want to speak to those of you who are thinking...

• •

"Hold Up... What IS Personality Marketing, Again? I'm confused."

In order to best clarify what personality marketing is, I should tell you what it's NOT.

Personality Marketing is *not* the same as "personal branding."

I thought I should be clear about that because the term "personal brand" is *so hot right now.*

Everybody's talking about how you need a personal brand to get ahead in your career.

So in response, many of us dutifully set out to create blogs, logos, "branded" photos for social media and all the other aesthetic elements of branding that seem like a really big deal at the time... *until we realize that **spending endless hours on all of that stuff didn't make us any richer** or better off than we were when we started.*

Don't get me wrong; developing a clear and strategic brand identity is a good thing...

...but it's what you DO with that brand that makes you money. Personality marketing means thinking *beyond* grapics and logos and getting *crystal clear* about **what makes you different** from the others who sell what you sell.

It means finding and putting to use the bits and pieces of **your unique story** that have the most potential power for persuasion.

It means being strategic about **the way you deliver that story** (or your "performance", if you will) so that it's engaging, entertaining, authentic, compelling and irresistible.

It means putting YOU out into the world as a teacher, expert, authority figure, thought leader and/or entertainer-- **using strategically created content to drive the right audience *into*** *and through* a **carefully crafted customer journey** with YOU as their trusted guide.

It means creating a **meaningful and lasting relationship** with your audience so that they 1) fall in love with you, 2) fall in love with your product/service, and 3) come back for MORE products and services in the future.

And you know what's AWESOME about doing this?

If you want to, you can set things up in such a way that you **make money WHILE you build your audience**-- so you can bootstrap the growth of your empire and (if you're REALLY good) even *turn a profit from day one!*

I say this because I want you to know that **there is nothing standing in your way.**

Not money, not technology, not *anything.*

You could start doing this *tomorrow* if you wanted to.

And you *should.*

*Because it's the **greatest.***

• •

Why Personality Marketing is the Greatest Ever and Everyone Should Do It

Maybe you've heard of sales funnels before. You might even have one. Or seven. I don't know.

Maybe you've tried social media marketing and/or email marketing.

Maybe you've even run some paid ads.

But if you haven't gotten the results you wanted from those efforts,

I'm guessing you *haven't* yet experienced the magic of personality marketing.

How is it different?

Personality marketing works because **it's created *by* real humans *for* real humans**.

> It's marketing with *enthusiasm*, with *empathy*, with *humor* and with *heart*.

> It puts *people* above *processes* and *stories* above *systems*.

> It's the *online* equivalent of building an *offline* relationship, *without* losing that all-important personal touch along the way.

> It's the *humanity* and *sincerity of your content* that make all the difference, because if you can't make people *feel* things, it could prove quite difficult to convince them to *buy* things.

And now, more than ever, personality marketing is NEEDED because content saturation has made it HARDER THAN EVER to stand out.

Why?

Because if you're not nailing this stuff, there's most likely a competitor of yours out there who IS.

And if so, the customer will choose *that competitor* instead of *you*, any day of the week.

It's not personal. It's business.

And business IS personal.

Here's what I mean by that.

Our brains are *full of stuff* to think about.

Errands, work tasks, home tasks, family, health... the list goes on and on.

It's not personal if we ignore your posts on social media. It's (most likely) *not* because we hate you or think you smell or curse your very existence on the planet.

But it *is* personal how we choose who we *will* pay attention to.

We pay attention to people:

- If they make us think
- If they make us laugh
- If they ease our suffering
- If they solve our problems
- If they answer our questions
- If they surprise us
- If they make us feel understood
- If they inspire us
- If they motivate us
- If "hanging out with them" online makes us look cool
- If we find them attractive
- If we find them interesting
- If we *don't* feel bored by them
- If we *don't* feel annoyed by them
- If we feel like they really care about us
- ...and so on, and so forth.

In other words, if I choose *not* to pay attention to what you post online, it's not about *you* at all.

It's about *me*.

On social media, if it's not *instantly obvious what's in it for me* if I stick around and pay attention to your content...

...I'ma keep on scrollin'.

And so will you.

We have no choice!

Faced with far too many options to possibly compare each one, *we seek out reasons* to tune people out.

We're looking for reasons to ignore you and keep scrolling.

But when we see a familiar face in our feed?

A face we like, a face we trust; someone who we know would NEVER DARE to waste our precious downtime?

We're *thrilled* to hear from them!

If you can create the type of sales-driven content that can earn you that sort of respect and attention, **the growth of your business will become easier than you ever thought possible.**

Here are some of the benefits that many of us "personality marketers" are experiencing as a result of the content we're sharing online.

- We **don't have to justify our prices** or discount our rates to compete because our content generates *plenty* of demand
- Our content **attracts prospects to us** and qualifies them before they ever take up a moment of our time
- Our **sales conversations are effortless** and we can pick and choose who we'll work with because we have more qualified leads coming in than we could ever need
- Rather than sending out endlessly ignored media pitches, **media outlets approach us** to weigh in as industry experts because they've already witnessed the impact and value of our content
- We **attract wealth more quickly and easily** than we previously thought possible because our audiences eagerly await hearing about each new product or service we have to share with them

Doesn't that sound nice? It is, if I do say so myself.

But how do you actually accomplish all of that?

Super simple: **create awesome content and get that content in front of the right people.**

Aaaaaand repeat.

A lot.

And don't quit.

And get better.

And if you want to go fast, ads and funnels can help.

In the chapters to come, we'll get into more detail about all of those things.

Just do me *one* small favor, would you?

Should you choose to use the great power of personality marketing, use it with *(to drop a bit of Spider-Man parlance on you)* **great responsibility.**

Don't make people fall in love with you and then turn around and be a jerk and sell them crappy products and stuff.

Okay?

Okay.

Glad we had this little chat.

Now... moving on.

• •

The #1 Biggest Misunderstanding About Personality Marketing

The temptation I see lots of entrepreneurs falling prey to when they get wind of this concept is to think the answer is **posting pictures of their lunch** or random live videos of them wearing bunny ears for no apparent reason.

Some "more advanced" marketers still miss the mark, thinking that all they have to do to cash in on the power of their personality is **brazenly boast about their glamorous lifestyles.**

And while that can sometimes be effective, if you think that's what personality marketing means, *you're missing the point.*

Good marketing always has begun and always will begin with **a sincere and generous focus on your customer.**

It is essential that you understand this, or you will not have the success you're after.

Creating content that gives you customers what they want, AND helps you sell?

> *That's how you're going to cope with the dwindling attention span of today's consumer.*
>
> *It's how you're going to win their loyalty.*
>
> *It's how you're going to stand out as (wonder of wonders!) **an actual human** in a sea of cookie-cutter sameness.*

And it all begins with a magical element that I refer to as *nerdiness.*

Not your old-school, stereotypical "pocket protectors and band camp" nerdiness-- I'm talking about the subtle, yet powerful quirks, fascinations and obsessions that color and enliven our distinct identities.

*We're all a little "nerdy" about **something.***

And if there's anything we nerds love, it's finding the *other* nerds who love the things we love and feel the things we feel.

The problem with your typical *"lack-of-personality marketing"* is that the face of the brand (let's say she's a woman) is so focused on making sales that she hides that *precious nerdiness* away-- squandering what could have been one of her most powerful marketing assets.

Now, many of you will take this to mean my telling you *"all you have to do is act like a dork in your videos and people will buy from you."*

That is NOT what I mean.

If you do that and it doesn't come from a real, sincere place within you, **it will most certainly NOT be effective.**

My goal here is simply to show you how to capture (and profit from!) the persuasive power of your *most authentic self...* with the occasional hint of theatricality thrown in to juice things up from time to time.

Your authentic self is your most powerful asset because in a world of "me too" marketers, if you want to be the one chosen over your competitors, you have to position yourself as the better option-- **preferably, the BEST option!**

And don't worry. We're going to talk about *a lot* of specific things you can do to make that happen here in this book.

But before we do any of that, I'm going to say something SHOCKING.

Are you ready?

• •

My (Not So) Top Secret Agenda for This Book

CONFESSION:

I didn't write this book because I was bored.

I'm using my "Personality Marketing Ninja Voodoo Powers" on you *right now!*

(And so is EVERY successful nonfiction author you've come across, by the way... although some are better at it than others...)

I'm being transparent about this because my #1 reason for writing this book was to build a relationship of trust with you. I know that if I can accomplish that here, it could very well open the door to my selling you *more* stuff in the future.

That's why my goal for our time together here is to be so helpful and fun and lovable that by the time you're finished reading, you cannot *help* yourself.

You're going to want to work with me.

Or you're going to want to hang out with me, or tell your friends about me, or something.

That's my *super secret* goal, anyway.

Don't tell anyone.

In all seriousness, though, I see no reason for any of us to try to hide the fact that we have something to sell because if your product really is good, *there is NO shame in talking about it!*

You don't have to hide behind sneaky sales tactics, but you *do* have to understand that the more your audience feels like you have their best interests at heart, the more receptive they stand to be to your sales message.

How do you prove that you're one of the select few who actually *care* about the wellbeing of your audience members?

By actually *caring* about them!

The irony in personality marketing is that the more you do it, the *less* it becomes about *you* and the *more* it becomes about *your customer.*

The reason I want you to hire me to help with your marketing *is NOT because I'm greedy and want your money,* **muahahaaaa...**

I want you to hire me because I really, **seriously want to** *help you sell more stuff.*

That's what gets me up in the morning.

I know how it feels when your marketing doesn't work and you don't know why.

I know what a scary, confusing, lonely journey entrepreneurship can be.

I love, love, LOVE helping amazing humans get the amazing marketing results they deserve.

And I know that a book, by itself, is unlikely to get you all the way there.

After all, reading a book is just the beginning-- it's what happens after you *finish* the book that will determine your ability to **make money from the things we discuss here.**

If you want my help making that money (*and I hope you will, because I hope this book will prove to you that* **I really do know this stuff well enough to actually be helpful**), when we're finished I'll be very clear about how you can move forward and get whatever degree of support and assistance you desire.

Sound good? *Good!* Let's party on down to Chapter Two, then!

• •

Chapter Two:

How to Use Personality Marketing To Create an Army of Nerds

Who Will Geek Out About (and BUY Lots of Stuff FROM) You

Huzzah!

The Big Difference Between Rookies and A-List Industry Leaders

There's a pretty significant difference between the way rookies sell stuff and the way A-Listers sell stuff.

Rookies chase prospects all day long (and seldom "catch" them), while a-list *industry leaders attract prospects with ease.*

How? **With *content*, that's how.**

Their content "goes out in front of them" to make a positive first impression, preparing the prospect to welcome and even invite their sales message.

And while it's true that creating and sharing the right content in the right way is the key to getting that all-important "foot in the door", you should also know that *that's just the beginning.*

The right content *organized into the right sales funnel or customer journey* can get you through the door, past the gatekeeper, into the office and straight to the heart (and wallet) of your ideal customer, day in and day out, without your even having to lift a finger.

If you want your content to do the selling for you, *your primary job is to get really good at creating it.*

Sales-friendly content is engaging, informative and/or emotionally compelling, but also *strategically crafted to generate desire* for the product or service you sell.

So let's talk for a minute about three things you can do to make sure your content strategy actually stands to make you money (rather than just waste your time).

1. Content that makes money is built to *sell*.

One big issue I see with people who've really taken this

"personal brand" idea to heart is that they create all this great content so they can get followers and engagement and views, but they fail to realize that they might not at all be creating *customers*.

One of my clients came to me after she had built up a huge following around the inspirational quotes she posts. She felt confused as to why *those people weren't actually buying anything.*

Of COURSE they weren't buying anything!

Think about it-- when was the last time you saw an inspiring quote on social media and thought, *"that was great. I'm going to buy something from this person!"* ???

That's right. You can't remember the last time it happened, *because it has NEVER HAPPENED.*

Which is why this second piece is so important...

2. **Content that makes money is built around an idea or a lifestyle people find appealing-- one that is relevant to the product or service you sell.**

It all starts with a "big idea"-- a specific sort of lifestyle or topic that your content will be about.

And (this is VERY important)-- your big idea **cannot be** *"my product is the best."*

At least, not if the whole "media company/having your own show" approach is what you're going for.

Because **nobody would want to watch that show**, right?

Your big idea answers the question: *if your social media videos were a reality show, what would that show be about, in a nutshell? Who would watch it? Why?*

Think about what makes YOU special, what makes YOU entertaining, but also think about the product. What made you want to sell it? How is it different? What sort of lifestyle or transformation does it enable you to have?

Getting clear about your big idea is one of the MOST IMPORTANT TASKS you'll undertake as a personality marketer, so we'll discuss it more extensively here later on.

But right now, let's move on to number three:

3. Content that makes money is aspirational.

This is a little element of "secret sauce" that I call "after-ness", or the degree to which you appear to be the "after" to your viewer's "before."

This is absolutely crucial.

In your marketing, we need to send the clear message that **you're actually experiencing something your prospect wants to experience**, or they're unlikely to want to buy what you're selling.

That's why, as awkward and braggy as it feels, I'm always posting stuff on Facebook like "Dang, guys! I spend $127 bucks on ads today and I made $4781 back!"-- *because I know that results sell.*

We want to see the before and after.

We want to see proof that you're not just blowing smoke.

And **we need to be reminded over and over that *you're legit,*** because it's human nature to be skeptical. *People are looking for reasons not to trust you.* It's our natural defense mechanism.

So in a lot of ways, this is really the key: *you've got to figure out **what makes you an "after"** and how can we use your "afterness"* to paint a compelling picture of what life is like on the other side of buying your stuff.

By the way-- **whether we feel confident about it or not, we've all already got "afterness" to play with, at least to some degree.**

We've all accomplished something or experienced some sort of awesomeness in our lives that other people would love to accomplish or experience. It's just a matter of figuring out how to tell that story in an authentic, compelling way, and then of course using it to transition into a compelling sales message.

You ready? *Let's do this!*

Do This NOW

Write down your answers to the following questions:

1) Sales-Friendly *What about the content you're sharing creates or amplifies the desire to buy your product or service?*

2) Benefits-Driven *What kind of lifestyle is your ideal customer seeking when they buy similar products or services to those that you sell?*

3) Aspirational *What makes you an "after"? What could you do to more effectively convey your "afterness" to your audience?*

A Word About "Nerd"

Let's talk for a second about *nerdiness*.

I need you to know that I am a nerd, and so are you.

And so is your customer.

We all have random quirks and obsessions that make us who we are. We all "geek out" about something or other.

When I talk about "nerdiness", what I'm really talking about is *enthusiasm.*

And of course, I hope you know that *our spending flows where our enthusiasm goes--* **which is why the "nerdiness" conversation is so important.**

One of the most powerful truths I've discovered since beginning my journey with personality marketing is that *the more you embrace your quirks, your obsessions or the things that make you "nerdy", the easier it becomes to attract raving fans and eager buyers* with your content.

Now, why would that be?

The way I see it, the benefits of incorporating your unique brand of "nerdiness" with your marketing are threefold:

1. Because you're **having more fun**, *you'll have more patience* to stick it out when things get tough (which, of course, they will). Therefore, you'll be less likely to quit before things start to get really good.
2. Because **your content will be more interesting** due to your increased enthusiasm, people will be more inclined to pay attention to it.
3. Because your brand will **attract a more specific audience**, *your customers and followers will have more loyalty to you* (after all, we tend to fall in love with people who we feel are *just* like us, right?).

NOTE: It's important for you to understand that the type of "nerdiness" I'm talking about here *is not the kind of nerdiness where you hide behind a book and let the "cool kids" get all the attention.*

I'm talking about the kind of *wide-eyed obsession that makes you the BEST at what you do*-- and because you're the best, you deserve nothing less than A-list status in your industry.

To help you explore *your* nerdiness, let me ask you a few questions:

What 'stuff' can YOU not get enough of?

What do you watch shows about/read books about/talk to your friends about in your free time?

What's YOUR obsession?

Are those obsessions a part of your brand identity yet? *If not, why not?*

Maybe you're a computer nerd like Bill Gates.

Maybe you're a crafty nerd like Martha Stewart.

Whatever your particular brand of "nerdiness" looks like, I invite you to watch what happens to the engagement you'll get on social media when you *embrace* that nerdiness, *pump it up* and *put it in the spotlight* where it belongs!

• •

It All Depends on This...

Exploring the niche-ier, nerdier side of your brand can be helpful to do because in many ways (especially in the beginning) **figuring out a way to set yourself apart** is one of your most important responsibilities as a business owner.

With that in mind, I've got a few *very important* questions for you, and you should know that you answers could make or break your success in business.

No pressure or anything, though. ;)

Here we go:

> **What are you saying that nobody else is saying?**
>
> **What are you offering that nobody else is offering?**
>
> **Who are you serving that nobody else is serving?**

In a content-saturated world, *different* makes all the difference.

Now, some of you are fortunate enough to offer a product or service that nobody else in the world offers-- or maybe what you sell has a little competition, but your version of it has some **unique, proprietary awesomeness** that no one has yet been able to match.

But for most entrepreneurs, the questions I asked above can be quite difficult to answer.

Most of you are probably in the same boat as I am-- selling something your customer could also get from TONS of other places or people at a wide variety of price points.

So what do you DO about that?

Well, I hope you already know that *competing on price* is most often a losing battle. For most salespeople and companies, that's not going to be the smartest course of action.

I hope you also know that some people get paid a small fortune for the same product or service that other people would sell for a steal.

Why the discrepancy?

It has everything to do with *positioning*.

If you're using helpful content to position yourself as an industry expert, then you have to realize that the way you'll gain your "celebrity status" (*or **not** gain that status*) has a lot in common with how a high school teacher gains popularity among his or her students.

Think back to your experience in high school.

Which teachers did you really like?

What made you want to learn from those specific teachers instead of some (or most) of the others?

Was it because of their credentials and degrees, or was it simply the way they made you *feel*-- the *experience you had* while learning from them?

Naturally, the better we feel in a learning environment, the more information we are likely to absorb and apply effectively.

If my boring-sauce high school history teacher went live on Facebook every other day, would I watch it?

Heck NO, Elmo!

But if my hilarious AP Bio teacher were doing it, doing funky experiments with foot fungus like we did back in the day?

I would LOVE to watch that!

Here's the reality, guys.

The VAST MAJORITY of entrepreneurs are competing for business in a commodity market.

That means we're up against a LOT of other people who sell the same thing we sell.

It's scary.

And it's the reason *SO MANY businesses fail.*

We think, "If I just tell the world about my super cool product, they'll want to buy it, right?"

WRONG!

That might have been true in 1950, but today?

Not so much.

There's one tried and true principle of sales that you cannot afford to forget, and it's this: **people buy from people they know, like and trust.**

If you miss the boat on your personal brand and go "all product, all the time," **you don't give yourself the chance to create that feeling.**

You might sell stuff, sure, and if your product is unique enough, a "product first" approach can most definitely suffice...

But you're *still* not going to create that feeling-- you won't be creating that deeper relationship that might mean more sales, referrals and loyalty down the road.

Chew On THIS

If you start treating your business like a media company (*again, in the sense that your primary job is to create sales-driven content that people will actually WANT to see*), **you'll be much better equipped to build that sort of relationship.**

I hope that by now you understand that content (especially video) can be a VERY powerful relationship-building tool, but

ONLY IF you know how to make engaging, sales-friendly content.

The old "content for content's sake" model DOES NOT WORK, and it's why it makes me nervous when people approach me and say *"I don't have time for my marketing... can your team just do it for me?"*

Most of the time what I want to say in response to them is... *"Well, technically **yes**, we **could,** but..."*

"Marketing is how you get customers!"

"It's how you make money!"

"Are you sure you want to hand that MAJOR RESPONSIBILITY over to somebody who isn't *you*?"

The way I see it, sending the whole *"selling stuff shebang"* over to someone else (ANYONE else!) and saying "here's some money, go make me rich" is akin to sending your toddler off to boarding school and saying *"Call me when he's 18!"* as you skip merrily out the door.

Your business is YOUR baby.

No one will love it like you do, obsess about it like you do.

Nobody will understand your product or your customers as intimately as you do *(unless maybe you're dropping hundreds of thousands each month with a big-time agency)*.

So sure, you can outsource all you want-- just make sure you do so knowing that **sharing content WITHOUT a solid strategy or a unique brand identity could prove to be a big fat waste of your time** and resources!

The further removed you are from your content creation process, *the more difficult it becomes* to infuse that content with a distinct and compelling personality.

But here's the good news-- I really do believe that with a little coaching, it's possible for ANYBODY, no matter what they look like or where they come from or what resources they have-- to harness the "power of the personality" to command higher rates and generate massive demand for what they sell.

How do we do that?

Well, it starts by making sure we've got the right offer in front of the right audience.

Then, we mine your story for all the juicy tidbits that are going to be meaningful parts of a larger sales conversation.

We also figure out how to position you as the right sort of "character" so that you can give people a compelling reason to tune in to your videos and other online content *and get to know you and your product well enough that eventually they might want to buy.*

Then, we figure out how to put all of these pieces together profitably and at least to some degree, automate the process of turning strangers into customers.

After we master all of that, what's left on our to-do list?

World domination, baby!

• •

How to Best Harness the Power of Your Personality So That World Domination Will Be Well Within Your Grasp

If your aim is to be THE go-to expert/obvious choice/most trusted name in your field (and I hope it is, **because there's honor in the desire for excellence**)...

It's pretty simple, really.

If the person watching your videos, listening to your podcast, looking at your photos or reading your blog can become convinced that **you can give them what they need** *in a way that no one else can...*

...and then if you can use strategic storytelling to **heighten the tension, the urgency and the desire they feel** *to have that need met sooner rather than later*, it will become *very easy* for you to make a sale.

For example...

If I decide to hire a personal trainer, I have a TON of people within my personal and professional network who I could consider hiring.

Plenty of people could do a great job in that area, but only one of them can get their share of my money.

So how do I make that decision?

How do I choose the person I'm going to hire, and whether or not I'll even be motivated enough to hire a personal trainer at all?

Well, let's say the *reason* I want to hire a personal trainer is **because I'm trying to address a very specific issue**: abdominal separation as a result of my pregnancies.

What if a personal trainer *I had never before met or seen* showed up in my news feed with a video ad about exercises I should *stop doing* because they could be making my ab situation even *worse!*

Who do you think would jump to the top of my mind as THE person I should be hiring?

Even better-- what if her video ad were funny, approachable and sincere, and she reminded me of one of my best friends from college?

Would I be whipping out my credit card right then and there?

Heck YES, I would!

Because her personality *combined with* her specific, relevant, perfectly targeted sales message *showed up* and made me feel both **safe** AND **motivated to take action** all at the same time.

Let's not forget--, more than anything, what I'm buying is a *feeling*. A *solution* to a problem. An *answer* to a question.

And if someone steps up and says "here I am! I'm here *just* for you!"

That's powerful stuff.

We want to hire experts and specialists because we love the idea that our needs and desires are special and unique.

We love the idea of working with and learning from the *best*.

But what does "expert status" even mean?

It means that you need to be strategic about the way you make people *feel* during your marketing process, because it makes all the difference in the world.

The right personality marketing strategy should turn you into such an influential figure in your customer's life that when that moment comes that they want to buy something that's going to make them feel that certain way, *they won't shop around.*

They'll go straight to you.

They'll do that because *they've already associated you with the way they want to feel*; the result they want to get.

So here's the ultimate question for you as we get started here:

Who will you need to become **in order to be an "a-list" expert in your industry?**

If you don't know yet, that's ok. We'll explore it further as we go.

But do go ahead and start thinking about it, won't you?

The time for "becoming" begins *now*.

Chapter Three:
The Highly Embarrassing and Very True Story of How Nerdiness Saved My Business

Nerd's the Word

It's All Fun and Games Until Someone Loses Their MIND...

Remember how I started telling you the story of my marketing services company, NerdyGirl.co?

At the beginning, *our future was looking **very** sunny.*

The branding was working, the positioning was compelling and we had lots of early revenue growth and momentum-- *so much so* that a well-established venture capital investor took notice and stepped up to help us grow.

In fact, he was so ready to go on this journey with us that *he gave us 40 grand in seed capital.*

To me, that might as well have been 400 thousand-- it was WAY more money than I had ever spent on growing a business, in any case.

Based on our early numbers, we were making these insanely exciting multimillion dollar projections and **I was having visions of ringing the bell at the stock exchange** when we went public.

Armed with our 40k, I gave myself a trial-by-fire education in PPC ads. I ran ads on Facebook, Twitter, Pinterest, Google, LinkedIn, even Reddit at one point, recruiting what was supposed to be a massive, eager, commission-only salesforce and a killer pool of freelance talent for us.

The ads worked (or at least, it seemed that way at first).

People were clamoring to be a part of what we'd built.

Scrambling to keep up and learning as I went, I created this super-detailed training program for our salespeople with scripts and slide decks and detailed instructions about how to talk to people online and what to say in emails and everything.

I created all sorts of automated vetting and onboarding features for our freelancers, to keep them organized and make it easy to choose between them and assign projects to them.

I created super-intense conversion tracking and optimization systems to stay on top of which ads were performing and which weren't.

We were bringing in TONS of people, so I set out to build a big fat infrastructure to support what I was SURE was going to be a massive influx of client business once our sales force started rocking and rolling.

I was working **all the time** and things were moving so quickly that it took me *much longer than it should have to notice...*

Despite all of our recruiting, onboarding, training and accountability efforts, I was the only one who was bringing in clients consistently.

Our salespeople were dropping off the map faster than we could bring them in and train them, and no matter what we tried, *we couldn't seem to turn it around.*

In other words, I had gotten so excited about *scaling it* that I completely forgot to *nail it* first.

...whoops.

Wahhhhh wahhhhh. (That was me making a sad trumpet sound).

All the investment money was gone, and there was no way to sustain our expenses with only me out there bringing in new client accounts... **not even close.**

Not to mention, I *hated* one to one networking and prospecting... *and* with three little boys at home to take care of, **I didn't have the time to do it** even if I DID enjoy it!

As you might imagine, *I was getting pretty desperate.*

For months, I learned everything there was to know about marketing and selling, but I could not figure out how make a commission-only workforce *work* for the business model I had built.

So I did what any desperate entrepreneur would do. **I hustled my butt off.** I networked every chance I got, and built us a pretty solid little client base, tried to stay afloat.

If I couldn't get other people selling, *at least I could sell*, right?

It was going to be okay... *(I thought to myself while crying into my Diet Dr. Pepper...)*

Except I was working ALL the TIME.

I had no time for my boys, let alone my husband, I was exhausted and **I felt like a big fat failure.**

But I'd been there before. *I could muscle through.*

Until one very depressing Christmas Eve when I found out that **my "muscling through" time had come to an end.**

That night I was sitting down with my investor and our accountant, looking at the numbers, and in so many words, what he said was-- *"this is not a business I want to be a part of. This isn't working."*

I had prepared for him to say that, though.

I put my most confident face on and I said, *"This is temporary. I will turn this around, and when I do, we can pick up where we left off, right?"*

I didn't expect him to say no... **but he did.**

Even worse, he kinda laughed at me a little.

One of those smug little chuckles, you know?

"*I don't think you understand, Brittany,*" he said. "*This is not going to work. There will be no more investment capital. For your own good, you should probably just shut it down.*"

It felt like the floor has just fallen out from under me.

That was my SHOT, I thought-- my *one shot* at creating something *truly spectacular,* and I blew it.

I was *destroyed.*

The next few months were a blur.

Making painful phone calls to people I owed money to...

...trying to get them to hold on a little longer because we were broke...

...having to tell my team I couldn't pay them until we could get some more cash...

...trying not to take it personally when one by one they jumped ship...

...clinging desperately to the floundering remains of my income but knowing that I had already reached the upper limits of my existing network and there weren't any more clients to be had...

It seemed like there was no way out. Like I'd fallen into a bottomless pit.

UNTIL...

One day, I was driving home after dropping my boys off at school, and it was like a lightbulb came on, and I thought, "*wait a second-- if I can't scale a sales force, what I CAN scale is ME...*"

"*I know how to write scripts... I'm a playwright, for goodness sakes; I can make videos! I know I can sell in person-- why shouldn't it work on video?*"

So I tried it... and *I failed at that, too.*

At least, it felt like I did.

I was super awkward on camera.

It was not at all like the stage.

I didn't know where to look, what to do with my hands, or even what to say, really.

My videos were unprofessional, boring and **not at ALL compelling enough** to sell our marketing services.

So I researched obsessively and *I did everything the "gurus" told me.* I put this word here and this word here and built a sales funnel just like they told me to. I created super-complicated retargeting campaigns to make sure NO ONE slipped through the cracks.

I dipped into our business line of credit to buy some more ads-- this time, just to get clients.

And... *crickets.*

And *crying.*

More money gone. More self-loathing. Thousands of dollars in ad spend down the drain.

But I refused to give up. I had no other options. I would scale my business with video or...

...or, nothing.

*I was going to figure it out. **Period.***

I suspected that my mindset needed some serious repair work, so (despite not being at ALL financially "ready" to do so) **I hired a coach** to help in that department.

And things started to get a LOT better, really quickly.

Just a couple weeks in, **I booked 12k in new agency business** in a single day.

I thought to myself, "Wow! This coaching stuff *works!*"

So I hired another coach to help me troubleshoot my funnel.

And one day that coach said something that **I will never forget:**

"The more YOU you become, the more your perfect clients are going to be attracted to you."

...WHAT?

Duh! *How had I not thought of that before!*

Of COURSE my videos weren't working! **They were SO BORING!**

I was so busy trying to do things "right" that I forgot to be ME.

There was nothing unique about my message or my content. *Nothing special.* I was saying the same old tired stuff everybody else was saying. I was giving people NO REASON to pay attention to me instead of the thousands of other people out there selling and saying the exact same thing.

Selling in person was so much easier because I could actually act like a *human*-- not some lifeless content-creating robot.

So I decided that day-- *forget looking fancy and polished and professional...*

I'm just going to have some *fun.*

I'm going to think back to theatre school and apply all the fun stuff I learned back then.

And what's more...

I'm going to make videos that are cooler and more real and more fun to watch than *everybody else's videos.*

I'm going to do what the musical theatre nerd in me absolutely *longs* to do...

I am going to make people *feel* stuff in my marketing.

*And you know what? They **did** feel stuff.*

And all of a sudden... I started SELLING stuff.

Easily. **On autopilot.** *Finally!*

The more I did it, the easier it became and the more people wanted me to teach them how to get the amazing results I was getting from my videos...

...which is exactly what you bought this book to learn, right?

Well, how about I go ahead and tell you right now?

• •

The Secret Sauce That Makes Personality Marketing Work

Want to know the "big secret" I discovered that saved my business?

I'll tell you what it's NOT...

When it comes to creating content that sells, *it's not about the tech.*

> *It's not about fancy cameras or sound equipment or software.*

It's not about hiring a big fat entourage to help you get stuff done (although admittedly, now that I can afford one, it's AWESOME-- but I can afford mine BECAUSE this stuff first worked without them…)

It's not about lighting or lucky breaks or a picture-perfect face or figure…

I mean, I know I'm pretty hot stuff, but… I'm not THAT hot.

No, the REAL secret was something MUCH less obvious than any of those things.

In fact, I discovered that the LESS I WORRIED about "looking just right" and the more I focused on having FUN and being MYSELF in my videos, the *better* they started to perform for me!

I understand now that this is the case because BEING YOU makes it *so much easier* to create a real sense of connection in your marketing.

It allows you the freedom to deliver your message *so powerfully, so sincerely and so enthusiastically* that **they cannot ignore you** and you **cannot be copied or replaced.**

So here's my message to you, if you're feeling inadequate, like you don't "deserve" to big a *big flippin' deal* in your industry…

Quit worrying about HOW to do this and begin by becoming WHO you need to BE to do this-- because that is *infinitely more powerful* than any marketing tactic you will ever try.

Trust me… I've tried them all.

After implementing EVERY "ninja marketing secret" in the book and getting NOWHERE, *nerdiness* was the secret sauce that finally saved my business.

I found a way to harness my uniquely nerdy passions for advertising, storytelling and performing to carve out a special niche for myself, helping people understand a new idea that *nobody else* was quite explaining all that well...

What *was* that new idea?

You guessed it!

PERSONALITY MARKETING, yo!

And I can tell you from experience, when you find that "special something" that serves a very specific group of "special someones" in a way that *nobody else* is serving them?

You WIN.

● ●

What's Changed Since That Soul-Crushing Christmas Eve

After I let go of my self-loathing and mental garbage and **started creating content that felt like ME** *(the new-and-improved, happier, more confident and SUCCESSFUL me, I might add)*, I started to see the results I had been dreaming of all along.

And I've got to say, those results were (and still are!) *absolutely amazing.*

My conversion costs outperform industry norms nearly *every time* I launch a new ad or sales funnel...

The better I get at teaching this stuff, the more consistently *my clients* are seeing similar (if not better!) results...

My ads and funnels are consistently (and in many cases, MASSIVELY) profitable, which means that I've been able to hire my "dream team" and new "work besties" to help me mastermind our rise to world domination...

Because I *have* that dream team, I can *slow down* and actually enjoy my life (recently I spent a full week on an Alaskan cruise *with almost no internet access* and we STILL made a profit, even though my team had to put out some MAJOR tech fires for me while I was gone)!

And you know what the even CRAZIER thing is?

Now, for the first time, I finally feel like I'm **doing the thing I set out to do** in the first place: help my peers to *sell more stuff, make an impact and just plain BE HAPPIER!*

How do I know it's working?

*You guys tell me **all the time!***

Every day, I hear from members of my audience who are thanking me for the results they've achieved from what they've learned in my free content ALONE-- but they're not stopping there!

They're reaching out, hungry for *more!*

They're telling my team that they're *more than happy* to pay large sums of money for my help with their marketing, because they *already trust me that much.*

> *They don't need to be convinced.*
>
> *They don't need to get on a call with me.*
>
> *They don't need to check my references or look at my resume (which is sweet, since the only resume I have these days is the one I bring to musical theatre auditions...)*
>
> *They already know they want to hire me because they've been watching my videos and hanging out with me on social media.*

And sure, feeling a bit "internet famous" from time to time is a delightful perk/added bonus I enjoy as a result of my personality marketing efforts, ultimately it's not *really* about that.

It all boils down to one very simple thing: **building your "know, like and trust factor" at scale** by letting your *content* do the heavy lifting for you.

> *If you can do that, there's no limit to how much your business can grow.*
>
> *If you can do that, you don't have to spend the best years of your life chasing down leads.*
>
> *The leads (and sales!) will come to you.*
>
> *They'll tell their friends about you.*
>
> *And you'll wonder WHY in the WORLD it took you so long to start doing business this way.*

Let me say this one more time, to *really* drive it home:

If you want to scale a personality-driven business online, you **MUST learn how to create content that makes people feel like they know, like and trust you.**

See, most people get stuck at the "trust" part.

They're pretty good at creating content that shows they *know* stuff...

But the only problem is, *lots of people know the same stuff they know.*

If you want to stand out, your content has to not only prove that you're a trustworthy and credible voice in your industry, but it also has to make people feel like they KNOW you and LIKE you!

How do you do that?

Stick around.

You're about to find out...

• •

How to Avoid Making the Same Mistakes I Made

My biggest mistake as a new business owner was, in retrospect, quite common.

I didn't begin with a profitable, scalable marketing strategy.

> I *did* know how to position my brand.

> I *did* know how to recruit and build a culture and do all the "fun stuff".

> I *did* know how to sell in person.

> But I *didn't* have a marketing and sales plan that would get us clients at scale.

I did what most new entrepreneurs do. I thought if I threw enough money at my marketing, if I hired enough salespeople, *something* would stick.

That was my mistake.

All you have to do to avoid it is remember this:

*It's on **you** to sell your stuff.*

Not your sales team, not your ad manager, not your branding consultant, not your PR guru-- the buck stops with **you.**

And that's *scary.* I know.

But it's also kinda *awesome* when you think about it.

After all-- *if you can get **really good** at selling stuff?*

You can pretty much get **whatever you want** out of life!

Selling is psychology.

It's persuasion. It's relationships. It's parenthood. It's friendship.

It applies to everything we do.

Which *might just be why we sometimes take it so personally* when we're not having success with it.

When we fail, the temptation is to use it as proof that one of our deepest, most profound fears is real-- **the fear that we're not good enough and that we're not worthy of being respected, admired or even loved.**

I feel like this is a particularly dangerous temptation among entrepreneurs, because so many of us get into doing what we do *because we feel called to do something Amazing with our lives,* because we feel like whatever it is we sell is bigger than just a paycheck, it's a MISSION. **It's who we ARE.**

And when WHO YOU ARE doesn't make money, it's hard not to feel like...

"WHYYYYYYYY!?!?!?! What's WRONG with meeeeee?!?!?!"

I totally get that. I have **SO** been there. You *know* I've been there.

But **here's the problem** with that line of thinking:

You make **bad business decisions** when you're thinking that way.

You skimp out on stuff you need to spend money on, or you go the opposite direction and make rash decisions and *spend too much too fast*-- because **you're not thinking strategically, you're thinking emotionally.**

And of course, thinking emotionally about business isn't always a bad thing, but it certainly *can* be if you're not being emotional and SMART at the same time.

Which is why SO MANY successful business owners talk about how important mindset is.

Because the "*I need to prove I'm good enough so this needs to work nowwwwww*" decision is rarely also the smart decision. The smart decision is almost always going to be based on something a whole lot more concrete than that.

So here's the distinction that's going to help you snap out of insecurity mode and get back into strategy mode a whole lot more quickly.

From now on, henceforth and forever, I want you to think of yourself as a scientist.

A MAAAAAAD scientist!

Kidding.

Just a regular scientist.

Or a mad one.

I don't judge.

The idea is the same either way.

I want you to think about each new business decision as an experiment-- the purpose of the experiment being to test a hypothesis and gather data.

So many of us waste so much mental energy waiting for a plan that's guaranteed to work.

Guys, **there's no such thing.**

I can teach you what's working for me, other people can teach you what's working for them, and that can help, but only if you do the work and test variations of principles you learn until you get it just right.

Expect that sometimes your experiments will fail. Get okay with that right now.

Plan for it. *Budget for it if you want to!*

Because if you really expect to make a bajillion dollars on the first try... well, as much as we marketers love to tell you it's possible, it's just highly unlikely. **Because we don't know what we don't know... until we find out.**

You have GOT to get your message right first. Tactics may come and go, but *the real money will ALWAYS be in your message-- ***saying the thing that makes people want to buy the thing.****

Period.

How do you know if your message is right?

Well, you can hire someone like me to help you get it right, and/or...

You can *experiment*.

And then you can get really good at *listening* and *responding* to what the market is telling you.

Through their engagement and with their credit cards, **my audience told me who they wanted me to be**. *My audience told me what they wanted to buy from me.*

If you're determined to figure this out on your own, then by all means, do it!

Just do me AND yourself the EPIC FAVOR of remembering this: *the success or failure of your marketing experiments has **nothing to do** with the success or failure of **who you are** as a human being.*

No matter what happens, please know that YOU are not your business. Successful or broke, *you* are *magnificent. You are extraordinary. Anything is possible for you and you DO deserve to succeed, no matter **how many times** you miss the mark.*

• •

NerdyGirl vs. the Potato People

Can I tell you guys a secret about fear?

I used to think that **one magical day would come** when I didn't feel scared any more... when I just KNEW everything would work out perfectly in my business and I could take whatever risks I wanted and never have to worry whether or not they'd pan out.

So far, **that has NOT been the case for me.**

Doesn't matter how many 20k days I celebrate... *the fear doesn't seem to go away.*

In fact, in a lot of ways the potential for loss just gets **bigger and scarier** as we go.

I used to think that turning a profit from my ads would *fix everything* and I'd suddenly feel confident and successful and *chill* about my business at last.

But you know what?

I've learned that at EVERY STAGE of success, **entrepreneurship requires big-time bravery.**

Every day **I have to fight the urge to hide under a blanket** and read self help books until those confident, fearless feelings show up again...

...because some days, for whatever reason, *those feelings REFUSE to show up.*

But you know why that's okay?

Because *those feelings don't make my decisions for me any more.*

I no longer let my inner "potato people" get the better of me.

Who ARE "my inner potato people," you ask?

It's the name my husband Clark gave to the nagging, negative voices we all have talking nonsense in our heads, trying to hold us back.

The lazy potato person...
The anxious potato person...
The potato perfectionist...
The potato of mom-guilt...
The pressure-cooker potato...

We've **all** got them.

But we DON'T have to listen to them.

One of the major takeaways I got from my first coach was the idea that I could go ahead and start *thinking* and *acting* like a successful business owner *right now,* **despite** what those poo-faced potatoes were telling me.

I didn't have to *wait* for them to go away. I didn't have to *earn the right* to dream big or play big, either.

And neither do you.

Don't FOR A SECOND let your insecure "potato self" talk you out of doing *whatever is required* to create the MASSIVE IMPACT ON THE WORLD that you are MORE THAN CAPABLE of creating.

Even on days when I feel absolutely terrified by the new challenges we're taking on, I still get up and make videos and write and serve clients and do the things I committed to do, *because those feelings are not the boss of me.* ***I'm the boss of me!***

Which sometimes means saying "shut up, you stupid feelings. I do what I want!"

It's not easy.

Entrepreneurship is not for sissies.

But neither is *life, yo!*

Hiding from what scares you does NOT keep you safe; **it only keeps you small.**

So before we move on, I want you to promise me to *read this book bravely.*

Don't get stuck in "I can't do this, ads are expensive..."

"I can't do this, I don't have a fancy camera..."

"I can't do this, everyone will laugh at me..."

Nonsense.

After years of suspecting I would *never amount to anything*, I went from **broke as a joke to Queen of the Nerds**, practically overnight.

Personality marketing worked for me, it's working for my clients, and I really do feel confident that it CAN work for YOU too.

Just thought you might need that little pep talk-- you know, in case you were waiting for that magical *"day of eternal confidence and swagger"* to arrive before you started playing big.

Turns out, if you do, you might find yourself waiting forever.

So **let's NOT wait**, ok?

Let's dive in...

Write down your answers to the following questions:

Get clear on what *your* inner "potato people" are telling you (and challenge their assumptions:

What does your inner lazy potato person tell you to do about your marketing and sales efforts?

Do you agree that that's a good idea?

What specific, positive action could you take the next time said "potato person" tries to tell you what to do?

What does your inner anxious potato person tell you to do about your marketing and sales efforts?

Do you agree that that's a good idea?

What specific, positive action could you take the next time said "potato person" tries to tell you what to do?

Do This NOW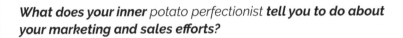

Write down your answers to the following questions:

What does your inner potato perfectionist *tell you to do about your marketing and sales efforts?*

Do you agree that that's a good idea?

What specific, positive action could you take the next time said "potato person" tries to tell you what to do?

What does your inner potato of guilt *tell you to do about your marketing and sales efforts?*

Do you agree that that's a good idea?

What specific, positive action could you take the next time said "potato person" tries to tell you what to do?

Do This NOW

Write down your answers to the following questions:

What does your inner potato of shame **tell you to do about your marketing and sales efforts?**

Do you agree that that's a good idea?

What specific, positive action could you take the next time said "potato person" tries to tell you what to do?

I know. *I get it.*

Defeating your inner "potato person" is **no easy task**, and it's something we have to continually work toward throughout our lives.

As much as I'd like to think that this little journaling exercise might be enough to change your sense of self-worth for the better long-term, *it's really just the beginning.*

I hope that someday we can meet in person and work through the **serious work** of *banishing your potato people for good* together.

Chapter Four:

How to Make Personality Marketing Work for Your Unique Situation

(Even If It Seems Impossible Right Now)

Ready?

Who is Personality Marketing For, Really?

At this point you might be wondering-- *"All of that 'rah rah' mindset mumbo jumbo is touchy feely and nice... but seriously... **is Personality Marketing a good fit for what I do?"***

Or maybe-- *"what's the big deal about being 'internet famous', anyway"?*

> *Isn't that just a vanity thing?*

> *Isn't it enough to just be good at what you do?*

To those, questions I would say...

> *In some cases, yes, but also... sometimes no.*

Going the "personality marketing" route isn't for everybody, nor is it necessary for every brand to have a face.

However, **you can't deny that it's a powerful thing.**

And not just for "online guru types" (coaches, course creators or information marketers) either.

Let's think for a second about some of the powerful (and often quite nerdy) personalities we associate with some of our favorite products and services...

1. Mark Zuckerberg
2. Rachael Ray
3. Chip Gaines
4. Ree Drummond
5. Dave Ramsey
6. The Progressive Insurance Lady
7. Oprah
8. Dr. Oz
9. Martha Stewart
10. Bill Gates

Having a *real human* to reinforce a brand's message is powerful, **no matter what the brand represents**-- especially if that human possesses a passion (a.k.a. nerdiness) for something we care about.

Was Steve Jobs' passion for innovation the "secret sauce" of Apple's success?

Was Tony Hseih's obsession with customer service what made Zappos such an e-commerce phenomenon?

Would the name "Goop" have *ever* been associated with a luxury lifestyle without Gwyneth Paltrow behind it?

I'm just saying...

I bring up these names because I want to make it clear that the things I'm about to share with you are **in no way exclusive** to any specific sort of business you're in.

You will LOVE **personality marketing if:**

- You want to put your awesomeness to good use
- You want to **make your mark on the world**
- You *don't have a ton of time* to be selling one-on-one
- You like to **teach, serve or just plain CONNECT** with other humans
- You want to sell **WITHOUT being sales-y or spammy**
- You like being in the spotlight (*even if it scares you a little*)
- You want to **set yourself apart** from your competition but you're not sure how
- You want marketing and selling to be FUN and EXCITING instead of OVERWHELMING and SCARY

Personality marketing can work for:

- The restaurateur who wants to **channel his/her inner Emeril** and turn deliciousness into dollars like a BOSS
- The brick and mortar store owner who wants his/her store to be **a BIG FLIPPIN' DEAL in the local community** (or even a franchise someday!)

- The **tech startup founder** who wants to stand out as a leader in his/her space
- The late bloomer who gets that it's never too late to **turn his/her wisdom and experience into a "legacy business"**
- The network marketer who's looking for a way to grow a customer base and a team **without having to harass or annoy his/her friends and family**
- The aspiring artist, consultant, speaker, author or online course creator
- The ambitious dreamer who's thought about starting a business, but i**sn't sure where to start**
- The freelancer who's looking to grow her business and **stand out from the teeming hordes of competitors** on Upwork or Fiverr or whatever freelancing platform is cool at the time you're reading this
- The service provider, salesperson, or coach who **needs to land high-level b2b clients or customers** in order to make the money he/she wants to be making
- The online course addict who's **stuck in information overload** and wants to clear out the clutter and stick to the stuff that's going to actually WORK
- *...anyway, you get my point. This stuff can work pretty much anywhere.*

• •

Can I Be Successful at Personality Marketing WITHOUT Video?

Maybe you're not super confident on camera.

Maybe you've got what some folks like to call "a face for radio."

Maybe you hate making videos, have no clue how to edit them, have no desire to learn how... nor the means to hire someone to do it for you.

If you fall into any of those categories, not to worry. There are still ways that you can build a name for yourself without having to create video content.

But before I tell you what they are, let me just say that *people of all shapes, sizes and attractiveness levels* **CAN do well with video IF they can create great titles, persuasive copy and compelling topics**.

The reason I so often recommend that people start with video is that *when people can hear your voice and see your face*, it becomes a lot easier to feel comfortable around you and your work because people will feel like they know who you are.

That said, *if you look like the unabomber, that might not be a good thing.*

You probably don't, though.

Give yourself some credit, right?

Keep in mind that today's video viewers often respond quite well to people who come across as more "real," so **don't let a little insecurity stop you** from creating video.

If you can swing it, **it's definitely worth a shot.**

That said, I know that *video just isn't for everybody.*

That's why I want to make sure you're aware of your other options, just in case.

The way I see it, outside of video, there are three additional options: *written content, audio content and images.*

As far as written content is concerned this will most likely take the form of a blog-- either hosted on your own site or on a platform like Medium.

If you're good at creating compelling written content that stands out, this might be enough for you to build an audience of loyal readers.

Do keep in mind, though, that you'll need to put in the work to **1) drive people to your blog, 2) convince them to subscribe, 3) keep them engaged** and **4) turn those readers into buyers.**

This can be harder to do with written text than it is to do with audio or video, but *it can be done in a pinch* (with some clever promotion and some really compelling writing.)

Next, **audio content**.

This typically takes the form of a podcast.

*Podcast listeners can be **very loyal and devoted** audience members.*

Also (I heard a statistic about this somewhere or other), apparently podcast listeners are more likely to buy stuff than blog readers are.

Finally, *depending on what industry you're in,* **you can create a name for yourself using images alone.**

This might be the most *difficult* of the three alternatives, but with some real talent and creativity it can be done.

If you're an artist or a photographer, for example, this might be exactly the right avenue for you.

Sharing your work on visual platforms like Instagram or Pinterest could help you build a following IF you're strategic about SEO, networking with influencers, follower growth strategies and hashtags.

In the end, though *(and this is true no matter what sort of content you're producing)* your success will mostly depend on the *quality and persuasiveness* of your content and the message it delivers.

If your content is good, it's MUCH easier to get people to pay attention to it.

If it's not so good, it will probably get better with practice.

Either way, creating content at ALL will get you a whole lot closer to success than just *sitting around **thinking** about creating content!*

So START CREATING!

Don't worry about the specifics too much.

Play to your strengths.

Do the things you *enjoy doing* and can CONTINUE to enjoy doing for months or even years while you build your following and build your credibility.

If you want to speed up the process, you basically have two options:

1) create a piece of content SO AWESOME that it goes viral; and/or
2) pay to promote your content.

Only one of these items is within your control. I'll let you guess which one that is...

FUN FACT: "Going viral" is not necessarily all it's cracked up to be.

Not unless your piece of viral content actually SELLS things for you.

And viral content is rarely effective, sales-wise.

On occasion, ads do go viral... but I find it's best not to try to force it. Just create the most engaging, sales-friendly content you possibly can and you never know... *you could get lucky.*

In the meantime, you might as well start running ads and *create your own luck.*

We'll talk more about that later on. For now, let's speak to another common obstacle that plagues would-be personality marketers...

• •

How Do I Get Over My Fear of Being On Camera?

The way I see it, this is really a self-image issue.

If you don't feel confident about the way you look, sound or come across on camera, it's difficult to want to film yourself.

I get that.

But here's the deal: the only way to get around that fear is to *decide you're not going to even give it the time of day.*

Here's the thing about emotions like fear: *there's no need to go through some big, involved process to "get over" it.*

Like we talked about earlier-- you might *never* get over it, and **that's okay.**

The more you feel like you have to *fight your feelings* or *resolve your feelings*, the more *stressed out* you're going to be, **which does not at all help** the situation.

Have you ever heard the famous quotation, "feel the fear and do it anyway"?

Well, that's exactly what you need to do with video!

The more you push through that fear and just DO it, the more comfortable you're going to feel. If you wait for the fear to go away before you start, you never will.

One thing you can do to make the camera less scary *(and even if you're **not** afraid of being on camera, I recommend you do this)* is to pretend the camera is someone you love.

Don't think about who might watch the video later or what they might think, just pretend it's not a camera at all.

Pretend the camera is **someone awesome.**

Best case scenario, you would be envisioning your ideal customer right there inside of that camera lens, just *loving you* and *hanging on your every word, gripping their credit card in suspense for the first moment they're going to have an opportunity to buy something from you.*

That's the best way I know to give an authentic, magnetic performance.

Quit thinking about *the way you look* and think about *the way you want THEM to feel!* Forget about YOU and put your focus on MOVING people!

Get excited about it!

The more excited you are, the more excited your viewers are going to be.

Enthusiasm is the antidote to fear. **Pass it on!**

• •

Can I be persuasive on camera if my personality isn't all that dynamic or entertaining?

Listen up, my friend, because **this is important:**

SO MANY OF MY CLIENTS feel *so concerned about* doing this stuff "right" that they lose sight of something *WAY more important-- **feeling GOOD** during the process!*

You can't be successful for long if the person you are on camera is totally different from the person you are in real life.

It won't feel good to you. *You'll feel like a phony.*

So if you're out there being yourself *(the most enthusiastic and energetic version of yourself, of course)* and some people don't like it? **Who cares?** *Those people were never going to buy from you anyway!*

Don't be afraid to put *the real you* out there because the right people will love you for *exactly who you are*.

You don't have to be an entertainer. You don't have to be fancy. You don't have to be polished. In fact, you'll be easier to relate to if you're *not*.

I don't want you to fall prey to the misconception that you have to be goofy or ostentatious or outspoken to be effective on camera, either.

There are MANY different ways to persuade.

Here are a few **"introvert friendly persuasion tools"** that come to mind for me right off the bat:

- Acceptance
- Empathy
- Patience/Listening
- Intuition
- Peace of Mind
- A courageous sense of calm and quiet
- Thoughtfulness/Insight

And that's just the beginning.

There are a lot of deeper emotions that I don't get to tap into nearly as often because I'm so used to being a spaz. That's not at ALL the only way (or even the best way!) to make a sale. It's just one of many equally awesome options that are available to you, should you choose to use them.

That said, there are two elements of your on-camera persona **that will almost ALWAYS make a difference**, no matter what it is you're selling, and they are:

1. Energy, and
2. Enthusiasm.

Those things are worth working on, because they *do* pay off.

But remember-- **you don't have to bounce off the walls to convey those emotions, either.**

You just need to "pump up the volume" a bit on the *you* that already exists, so your viewers can feel (and hopefully begin to share) your passion for what you're all about.

• •

How does this stuff work for realtors or other types of service providers?

Like a lot of things, selling real estate and/or professional services usually begins with some **good, solid outreach to your existing network**, or sphere of influence.

I'm sure you know that already.

The real challenge comes when it's time to **move outside of your sphere of influence** and start selling to people you don't yet know-- *because everybody and their dog knows someone who can do what you do already, right?*

Since you've already heard my story, you know I have *totally* felt that pain. **The struggle is REAL.**

So the question is-- *what can we do to get people you DON'T know to pick YOU* rather than just following their social guilt and hiring their next-door-neighbor's nephew?

Do you think the usual stuff (you know, *the cookie cutter website, boring business cards and stale, overused and joyless Facebook photos everybody else seems to share*) are enough to set you apart?

No way, Jorge!

To move beyond your current sphere of influence, you need two things: you need to get *tenacious* and you need to get *creative*.

Now, as far as tenacity goes, I'm assuming you already know how to hustle and cold call and knock on doors. *I'm not the one to help you with that.*

I will, however, tell you a quick story about one of my favorite examples of this type of tenacity, though-- just to get your creative "tenacity juices" flowing.

My mother-in-law, a realtor, once had a buyer who wanted a house on a very specific street. Only one problem... *no one was selling a house on that street!*

So my sales-savvy MIL did what any self-respecting sugar addict/grandma would do.

She went out, bought some nice-looking cookies, and left them on the doorsteps of everyone on the block with a note asking if they might be willing to consider selling.

Sure enough, *it worked.*

Now, I'm no math whiz, but given my limited knowledge of real estate commissions I can only imagine the ROI when you compare what she spent on cookies to what she made from representing both the buyer *and* the seller on that deal!

But again, **that hustling/prospecting-type stuff isn't my strong suit.**

If you want to get **creative** with your message and your online marketing strategy, though? *I can help you there.*

And I'll tell you right now, here's what it's about-- it's about figuring out *what you can say that nobody else is saying*-- what you can offer (that people are actually going to care about) that nobody else is offering.

I'm not just talking about, "*Look at me! I can get you top dollar for your house! I'm reliable and trustworthy and nice!*"

Yay for you! I expect that.

If I don't get that from you, you're not doing your job.

We've got to go deeper.

We've got to have more fun with this. I'm talking about turning you into a celebrity so it's IMPOSSIBLE to forget you and IMPOSSIBLE to resist your awesomeness and charisma.

But in your case, even *that* might not be enough. We need to create an *irresistible offer* that will **speak louder than the noise** and be **too compelling to ignore.**

I say this because it can be harder to turn a professional services brand into a "lifestyle brand".

For example, people don't tend to tune in to hear every word their favorite realtor has to say, no matter how much fun they have going live to talk about the *oh-so-glamorous gossip* from the MLS.

I mean, it's possible...

But it's rare.

And you don't necessarily need the same kind of "celebrity status" or following that people in other industries do to be successful.

However, you *can* **channel your personality into creating one powerful signature offer, service or message** and then **delivering that message in an engaging, compelling way.**

I've seen that done VERY effectively by service providers in even the "un-sexiest" of fields, so don't you go thinking this "personality marketing stuff" isn't for you.

It just might look slightly different on the tactical side.

With the right message and the right content, that "leads and sales on autopilot" dream *can* happen for you, too.

• •

How does this stuff work for brick and mortar or ecommerce businesses?

For ecommerce and brick-and-mortar store sales processes, the "celebrity" side of personality marketing is a tougher nut to crack, because we usually make those sorts of purchase decisions in a very specific way.

HOWEVER...

I still maintain that **a little "star power" can go a long way** in just about *any* business-- just take it from the super-enthusiastic dude who's been showing up in all the commercials for a brick and mortar store called PC Laptops here in Salt Lake City for as long as I can remember. He's no stranger to the "power of the personality".

One thing I generally recommend that you brick and mortar

and ecommerce folks think about is this: *what's the personality of your ideal customer-- and how can you show up in a way that* **reflects that personality back to them?**

That's who you *(or whomever you choose to represent your brand)* must become in order to convey the most compelling message possible.

OR, for a truly memorable experience, you can **create a personality** *for your store itself* that's completely different from what your customer might expect.

You could be the next "Soup Nazi", for instance, replacing kindness and courtesy with melodramatic rudeness and weirdly demanding expectations for your guests...

...or you could go overboard in the opposite direction *(one of my favorite positioning strategies, by the way)* and **pile on the luxury** throughout the customer experience, leveraging every detail to make your customer feel like royalty from the very first moment you meet them.

My point is, **one of your greatest possible marketing opportunities lies right there within your customer experience**.

If you can imbue *that* with a remarkable (different/unusual/exciting/memorable) personality, your customers *will* keep coming back for more.

And if you do a *really* good job at this, they'll bring their friends. And *they'll* bring *their* friends.

And, well, that's the dream, yes?

I thought so.

• •

How does this stuff work for network marketers?

I *love* network marketers!

You guys are so much fun to hang out with-- you're just so *social!*

That's probably why so many of you feel drawn to this marketing style.

Well, that and the sneaking suspicion that **what worked for your upline may not work quite so well** any more...

When I hear from you guys *(and I do-- a LOT--)* the main thing you want to know is, **will Personality Marketing work for you, with all of the compliance issues and other challenges you have to deal with?**

Well, let's talk about that for a minute.

Here's the deal: if you're looking for help doing home parties and booth thingies and all that business, I'm not the one to help you. *That's not my world.*

But if you want to talk **online marketing**-- and I'm talking the GOOD kind, not the obnoxious kind that makes everybody want to unfollow you-- then listen up.

If there's one thing I know about marketing, it's this-- **I know how to create content that makes people want to listen to you.**

And pay attention to you.

And like and comment and share and come back for more.

The great thing about personality marketing is that it enables you to "make friends" at scale.

And as a network marketer, making friends (a.k.a. building your *network*) is **your most important job**, right?

Here's how you make friends and influence people with online marketing.

Are you listening? It's simple.

YOU HAVE to think beyond the product.

I mean, don't get me wrong, if you're super tenacious and shameless about putting products in front of people over and over every single day, you could do pretty well.

But if you want to build *real* relationships, *you've got to think differently.*

You've got to make your message **bigger than your product** because when you're selling the same thing as thousands of other people, *you cannot afford to put yourself out there the exact same way as they are.*

Because here's one thing I know for sure:

People WILL get sick of hearing about your products day in and day out. **But there's one thing we never get sick of, and that's *great content.***

Now, *reality check time.* So many people think they're sharing great content, but really they're not.

Either their headlines are crap, or their videos are so boring that nobody watches them, or when they get on camera they look super uncomfortable, which makes US feel uncomfortable-- *so be careful here.*

If your stuff really is as good as it could be...

Well, that really *could be* all you need.

Many of the network marketers who come my way feel like this isn't for them because the paid ads and fancy funnels freak them out a tad-- so if that's you, let me say this...

You might not need paid ads at all.

You might not need your own website.

You could have more success *just* by creating better content.

Could all the fancy ad and funnel stuff help you? Absolutely, it could BUT you can also keep the process SUPER-SIMPLE while you build things up a bit.

And if you're STILL not sure marketing automation can work for direct sellers, you're welcome to check out A-List Industry Leaders like April Marie Tucker, Tabitha Blue, Hayley Hobson and Sarah Robbins-- look at how *they're* getting the results they're getting...

And let me know if you're still skeptical after that.

HINT: You won't be.

• •

Yeah, but... I don't have fancy equipment/Yeah, but... I don't know how to edit video/ Yeah, but... I don't know how to do captions/ Yeah, but... I'm not all that attractive or interesting to watch...

If any (or all) of those concerns are getting in your way right now...

You MUST *CHILL.*

None of those things are prerequisites to your success *unless you decide they are.*

Many of my clients (and even some of my peers who are making *millions* right now) are *still making their videos with their phones.*

Many of them forego editing altogether and just start out making live videos while they get the hang of things.

Some *don't even want to make videos at all--* so we're exploring other options, and that's TOTALLY FINE.

The point is-- they're *starting.* They're not waiting for the "perfect circumstances" to arrive.

Some of my early videos were crapTACULAR, guys! Sometimes, they *still* are craptacular!

But that's *okay.*

The more room you allow yourself for imperfection, the more confident you'll feel (and the more compelling your content will be!)

Does a nice camera help?

A rockin' body?

A perfect smile?

Maybe... maybe not...

I mean, I know *my* body is one fine specimen (*I write as I stare down at my Jabba-the-Hut like pregnant belly...*) but I'm guessing you felt drawn to me for something other than my striking glamour and supermodel-ness...

Am I right?

I've said it before and I'll say it again-- the best way to position you as an expert is NOT with fancy bells and whistles, stunning good looks or movie theatre quality cinematography.

The most important element of ANY personality marketing strategy is **the value you provide the customer** and **the way you make them feel** as they listen to the stories you tell.

Think about some of the famous entertainers you know and love.

Rebel Wilson or Jack Black, maybe?

They're not polished or perfect either, but we LOVE them! *Because they OWN who they are* and they make us feel comfortable owning who WE are, too, right?

Yes. I AM right. **Thank you for thinking so.**

So do yourself a favor and *step outside of your self-doubt* enough to be 100% invested in the invisible prospect on the other side of the camera lens.

As soon as it becomes more about THEM than it is about YOU, you're going to feel a million times better.

> As long as you're stuck in "am I good enough/ready enough/cool enough" mode, no amount of tech wizardry can help you...
>
> *But we ALL can be selfless.*
>
> *We ALL can tell stories.*
>
> *We ALL can show empathy.*
>
> So **start there, and the rest will come.** Every time you practice, you'll get better and better.

No excuses, people. You're too cool to make excuses. Knock it off.

• •

Yeah, but this is going to cost a ton of money, huh? Ads, fancy software, etc etc etc...

Ok. The money issue.

Elephant in the room. Let's address it right now.

Am I a big fan of growing businesses with paid advertising?

ABSOLUTELY.

'Cause I like to go FAST when I can.

That said, there are *plenty of ways* to make your content work for you WITHOUT ads, without expensive lead generation systems, CRM stuff, a fancy-schmancy websites, trade shows, networking events...

Remember, **it's the *principles* that matter most.**

It's the *psychology* of all of this that makes the difference.

And you can win with a solid knowledge of buyer psychology, **no matter *what* the tactics look like.**

Might spending money on certain things help you achieve more rapid success?

Sure-- but personality marketing CAN work on a barebones budget, too.

That said, there are **a few "money-related thoughts" you might want to consider** as you get started, because one of the best ways to *ensure you're even in the right business in the first place* is to evaluate the profit potential of that business.

If you're still in the "weighing your options" stage of your entrepreneurial journey, you might want to consider the answers to the following three questions:

1) How much is a customer worth to you?

The *more you can afford to spend* to at least break even getting a new customer, *the more ads you can buy* and *the more you can invest in your marketing* in general.

Assuming your content and/or your ads are good enough to make a positive impression, then **a higher marketing spend should equate to more and more influence, impact and income** for you.

Keep in mind that *even if you don't break even right away*, with diligent nurturing and follow-up efforts, *you could still create a profitable customer relationship long-term.*

That's why savvy marketers tend to be more concerned with the *lifetime value* **of a customer** as opposed to the *immediate value* of a customer.

That said, the lifetime value of *your* customers only matters **if you can afford to be patient** enough to stick with them and continue marketing to them over the long term. Which leads me to the next question...

2) How long can you wait before you need to make a sale?

This question is less about customer value and more about *cash flow*. If you don't have any money in the bank, **your need to make a profit *quickly* becomes much more urgent.**

As fun as it is to do the work of "scaling your empire" with ads and funnels, if there's not a penny to be found, that can be tricky to do.

How will you access the funds you need to grow?

One thing that's proven to be true about us humans is that if we want something enough, we tend to become quite resourceful.

So if you want to rock and roll with this stuff and you want cash in the bank to make it happen, then do what you have to do and *go make some cash!*

> Start conversations.

> Show up and serve.

> Do more of what has worked for you before.

Of course, the *best, most fun and exciting* way I know to rapidly grow a large, lucrative following is to **build a sales funnel that's profitable on the front end**, which simply means that you set it up so that your prospect has the opportunity to buy a product (possibly even a series of products) from you *sooner rather than later.*

Is this **an easy way to make money?** *Heavens, no.*

In large part, your ability to turn a profit on the front end will depend on...

3) How intense is your prospect's need or desire to solve the problem your product/service solves?

This is an important question to answer because it's likely to dictate *the amount of money a prospect is willing to spend* on what you have to offer.

Can you "pump up the volume" on your customers' desire to buy by adjusting the way you *talk* about what you sell?

*You certainly can... and you **should!***

But no matter how great you are at writing persuasive sales copy, if you're weighing two business ideas against one another, I will almost always recommend that you **pursue the option where you see *the greatest, most intense need* for solutions, content, products and/or services.**

Chances are, **if there's a lot of intensity AND a lot of need, the potential for profit for you will be much higher** than it would be elsewhere, where what you have to offer might not be perceived as "that big of a deal."

The key to creating the money you need to enable you to create the impact you want to create is getting *crystal clear* about how you can make yourself *(and, by extension, your product or service)* seem as valuable as possible.

To do that, you MUST find a way to be DIFFERENT-- but not just different for difference's sake-- different in a way your ideal customer will actually CARE about.

Master those things, and you'll be *well* on your way.

• •

The Bottom Line: Will Personality Marketing Work for You?

As is true with *anything* in life, this stuff will work for you **if you choose to MAKE it work for you.**

You've got to take action.

You've got to do what you can with what you have.

You've got to learn from your mistakes.

You've got to be patient and you've got to do the work.

If you're waiting for your financial, physical and emotional "stars" to align, *you'll probably get left behind by the people who took advantage of this MASSIVE opportunity while it was still brand new.*

The answer to the "will it work for me" question **depends ENTIRELY on what you do next.**

With that in mind, what *SHOULD* you do next?

*Allow me to make a suggestion...***Let's start by really getting clear on your *positioning.***

Chapter Five:

How to Position Yourself As A Game Changer

(Even If You Feel Like A Big Fat Imposter Right Now)

Game On!

The Three Types of People We're Most Likely to Buy From

Having come to this point in the book, you might be feeling a little intimidated...

...or if not intimidated, maybe a little skeptical about whether or not "expert status" is *really* the thing you need to help you sell more stuff.

And you're right. It might not be.

That said, "expert status" is not *actually* what all of this is about. There are other ways to be an A-List Industry Leader without actually being the leading expert in this or that.

As it turns out, there are three distinct types of people we tend to buy from, and as I talk you through them, I want you to guess which one you think stands to be the most persuasive:

- The expert *(we buy from them because we trust them)*
- The icon *(we buy from them because we want to be like them)*
- The friend *(we buy from them because we can relate to them)*

If you picked "the friend," I would say that you're **absolutely right.**

Think about it-- who would be more likely to convince you to buy a certain car: *a good friend* who lives in the same climate, carries similar cargo and has the same number of kids as you have, *or a "car expert"* who could talk your ear off all day about the superiority of the engine?

The friend, right?

Which is EXCELLENT news!

What this means for you is that you don't have to be an "after" in the sense that you know everything and have achieved everything a human being can possibly know and achieve. You just have to have *confidence in the product or service you sell*, and the ability to convey your thoughts about it in a friendly, approachable way.

Let me give you an example.

Recently I spent $60 on some really cool laundry detergent thingies made by a company called Crystal Wash. Their ad took me to what looked like a blog post (but was actually an advertorial) by a woman who looked like she could easily be a friend of mine.

She talked me through the science of the product, why she loved it, why it worked and why it was going to save me time and money.

So I bought it.

It wasn't because I thought she was a laundry expert.

It wasn't because she was the most beautiful woman I'd ever seen.

It was because she reminded me of someone I knew, and in that case, that was enough.

So I don't want you to think that you have to be a BFD (big flippin' deal) for this stuff to work for you. *You don't.*

But just in case you DO want to be a BFD...

• •

How to Be Perceived as the Celebrity Expert You Were Born to Be

Want to be known as the best in your field?

A big piece of that is **making sure you look the part.**

We've already discussed, to some extent, the importance of "after-ness," which means YOU showing up as the physical representation of the *specific result or benefit or lifestyle* this customer is hoping to get from the product or service you're offering them.

Now I know that this idea might make you a little bit nervous, thinking *"...but what if I'm NOT an 'after'?* **What if I'm still a work in progress?"**

Well, first of all, stop worrying about that right now because we *all* are.

If you look hard enough at your life story, *you will find nuggets of awesomeness* that will enable you to position yourself as an "after" even if you're just starting out.

You can start by looking at **your cool accomplishments, your work history, your credentials, your education, or other "claims to fame" you might have that you can use to make sure people know (and make sure YOU feel CONFIDENT) that you're legit**.

If your plan is to *trick people into thinking you can deliver something you actually can't deliver*, let's definitely not work together, because **I prefer not to help butt munches like that make money** if I can avoid doing so.

Ok? Ok.

Assuming you're not a scammer, though, one thing you can start thinking about now is how to **use the design elements in your online presence** to convey the highest-possible degree of "after-ness."

Design, after all, can be a huge deal when it comes to positioning you as the best in your business.

And before you freak out about how much you think this is going to cost you, let me make it clear that great design doesn't have to be expensive. There are plenty of ways you can look awesome without breaking the bank.

Here's what you need to think about:

1. The exact types of images your customer needs to see,
2. How and where you'll display those images in order to send the right message about you.

Everything from the images on your website to the backdrop in your Facebook live videos *says something* about what people can expect from you, so it definitely merits some careful consideration.

Mostly, though, this step is about figuring out how to visually *tell the story of the transformation* you're prepared to offer your customer; **how to make it abundantly clear from the moment they lay eyes on your stuff that you've got something they want, and that they should avoid the temptation to get distracted and take action NOW.**

"The Right Way (and the WRONG Way) to Think About Personal Branding"

thebookonpersonalitymarketing.com/video-2

Just like I wouldn't be as likely to buy from a door-to-door salesperson who looked like they hadn't showered in three weeks, *I probably wouldn't be all that inclined to put someone like that on camera*, either.

Like it or not, **looks DO matter**, so if you're going to be the star of the show, *you've got to put your best face forward*. You do NOT have to look like a supermodel, of course, but you've got to be someone the viewer can 1) *feel comfortable watching* and 2) *be* *inspired by.*

If your looks aren't particularly "inspiring," not to worry. *The best looking candidate is NOT always the one to close the sale.* **As long as you at LEAST look approachable enough to fill one of the following criteria,** a nice persuasive sales message and a compelling offer should be more than enough to get the job done...

In order to sell effectively on video, it's quite helpful if you look like one or more of the following:

1. Someone the customer would want to *be/look/feel like*
2. Someone the customer would want to *hang out with/be friends with*
3. Someone the customer would want to *date/marry/ engage with romantically*

The reason this is so important is because whether you're buying tomatoes, Teslas or toothpaste, **what you're really buying is a reinforcement of who you are** or who you want to be.

Organic tomatoes? *I'm health conscious and/or care about the environment.*

Fancy car? *I'm a success. People should know.*

Bargain toothpaste? *I'm no fool. I'm a savvy shopper.*

When we buy from a certain person, the situation is no different. The people we choose to buy from, listen to, and watch reflect the people we want to be and/or be around.

This is not about giving you a makeover (although in some cases it couldn't hurt...) this is about figuring out how to make the most of what you have to work with.

Have a good side? *Film it!*
Hilarious personality? *Tell jokes!*
Have what they call a "face for radio"? *Use slides or animated explainer videos!*

There's a reason successful salespeople often drive fancy cars and take professional headshots-- they know that *when you look successful, happy and prosperous, people want to buy from you, listen to you and generally give you the time of day.*

That's why highlighting the things that make you look (and feel) your most confident will pay off on video, just like it would in an offline sales job.

"Just How Much Should I Share on Social Media?"

Building an online presence is different than managing your in-person presence. It requires a bit more strategy than your everyday friend-making activities, because people follow strangers based on *content* rather than mere *proximity* or *convenience.*

But do you know what I absolutely LOVE about what's happening on social media today?

Consumers are demanding more and more authenticity and transparency from the brands they follow.

In other words, **we don't always expect or need to see slick,**

polished, perfect images and videos from the people and companies we buy from. We want to buy from *real people--* and more than that, people we know and like!

Of course, it's easier to feel like you know someone *when they don't try to hide their imperfections.*

Which begs the question... "Just HOW imperfect should I be on social media?"

There's definitely a gray area here, and as marketers, *we need to be careful.*

Today, a lot of us do have some crossover between the social media accounts we keep for personal use and the accounts we use for business stuff, which makes it even more important to know the answer to this question.

After all, you don't want to brag too much or paint TOO rosy a picture, or **you might be perceived as arrogant or unapproachable**. BUT you ALSO don't want to be so self-deprecating or negative that you **lose people's respect**.

So how do you figure out *what to say and what NOT to say* to make sure you're making the right impression on social media?

Here are some elements you might want to consider as you craft, grow and maintain your personal brand on social media.

#1: Want It? Give It!

Let's say that maybe it's been just one of those *days.*

Maybe your kid took a sharpie to your couch and your favorite client decided to take their business elsewhere and somebody asked you if you were pregnant at the store *when you're most definitely NOT...*

For whatever reason, *you're feeling pretty crappy.*

One of the wonderful things about social media is that it makes it *SO easy to reach out to your friends (or fans or followers) for support* during moments like that.

And you should... *sort of.*

If you're using social media as a means of promoting a product or service, though, you have to keep in mind that customers don't like to "put their gold on a sinking ship", so to speak.

If you frequently complain on social media, it could have a negative impact on your perceived "afterness"-- not to mention on your outlook on life in general!

It's okay to tell the truth that things don't always look perfect in your world-- but being transparent and being a **total buzzkill** are two *very different* things.

So with that in mind, in those moments when you really need to reach out for support on social media, **why not give *others* the same kind of support that *you're* looking for?**

Not only should that help you feel better faster, but it will also help you look a bit more put together-- *like a giver, rather than a taker.*

So sure, tell the story about the sharpie and the grocery store, but remember-- it's highly likely that someone else out there could use the exact same words of encouragement you need, so *why not, as you share your story, also take it upon yourself to* **be the first to see the bigger picture?**

#2: Be VERY Careful With Criticism

I would say about **90% of complaints made online make the complainer look petty and bitter**. *10% (if that) make the complainer look smart.*

How do you know if you're the exception?

I would venture to say, if you're not sure, *you're probably NOT the exception* and your complaints and criticisms of other people and companies are really just **making you look like an insecure, "nothing better to do" troll.**

*The best way to build yourself up will **never** be to tear others down--* no matter who the people you're complaining about may be. If you feel inspired to take a stand about something, **take a stand for what you believe in** rather than spewing negativity AGAINST the things you DON'T believe in.

And remember, the best way to win in business is NOT by making other people look bad-- *it's by making YOU and the stuff you sell look GOOD!*

A big part of looking like an "after" on social media is showing up as someone who is kind, respectful and 100% *secure about their own awesomeness.*

#3: Attitude is Everything

As long as you have *the right attitude*, you can get away with **sharing just about anything** and still end up looking awesome.

Haven't done laundry in 3 weeks? *Party on!*

Gained 200 pounds of baby weight... 20 years ago? *No prob, Bob!*

Declaring bankruptcy? *You can STILL look like a winner...*

IF you have the right attitude about it.

You know what's *even more awesome* than social media stalking people who "have it all"?

Social media stalking people who don't have it all, but who will *cheerfully press on toward their goals* until they eventually emerge victorious-- **despite seemingly insurmountable obstacles.**

Now THAT's a story worth telling.

So yeah, tell it like it is. We'll be happy to hear it-- but only if you don't whine, complain or act all passive aggressive, trying to get people to say nice things to you because your life is soooo pitiful and hard.

Hope sells. **Hope creates believers.** *Whining does not.*

If you can muster a good attitude (and sometimes, even a sense of humor) about life's challenges on social media, you can come clean about any and all drama that might come your way-- and your friends and fans will love you throughout all the ups and downs you share..

The truth is, **people LOVE it when you come clean about what's imperfect about your life**... but *if you have a bad attitude, we do NOT love it.* More often than not, it just makes us uncomfortable.

And really, if the only way you can think of to feel significant on social media is to throw a pity party or talk trash about what somebody else is doing, **that's a pretty good sign that you're not actually contributing anything awesome** enough to stand on its own two feet-- *so why should people pay attention to you, anyway?*

Because they feel sorry for you?

*Is that **really** the kind of attention you want?*

I certainly don't want that kind.

#4: Remember-- It's Not About You

While sharing real, personal, human stories on social media can help strengthen the bond between you and your audience, you can *never allow yourself to forget* that when it comes to making the sale, it is NOT about you.

It's about giving your customer what THEY want.

So *anything customer-facing* that you share on social media **should have THEM in mind.**

The more you show up as the "interested person"-- the one who cares the most about a particular customer, who's passionately devoted to giving them whatever it is that they want and/or helping them to avoid whatever it is that they fear-- *the more they're going to care about what you have to say.*

As you do this, *you don't really have to talk about yourself all that much.* In fact, you don't even **really** have to talk about yourself at all, as long as you keep showing up and keep giving your people what they want.

One of my marketing heroes, Donald Miller from StoryBrand, puts this so simply. He says that in the story of your brand, *your customer is the hero and you are the guide.*

They're Harry Potter, you're Dumbledore. They're Captain America, you're Dr. Erskine. He teaches that *the big mistake most marketers make is in thinking THEY're the hero--* that the customer wants to hear all about their story, but they really don't.

They want to hear about their OWN story and how you can help make sure it has a happy ending.

That's exactly why when you become a client, we'll spend a TON OF TIME making sure your copy (**the words you use** in your ads, your emails, your videos, on social media and on your website) are written in such a way that when your audience hears them, they think, *"How on Earth did this person get inside my head?"*

That's what we're going for-- because it's a tale as old as time that **the marketer who best speaks the language of the customer is the marketer who wins**, and it is my job to help you become *positively fluent* in that language.

Every time you post something new, you should always be

asking, "*Will my ideal customer find this interesting/entertaining/ funny/inspiring?*"

While it can be helpful from time to time to be a little bit strategic about things like your **image** and your **design** and the **tone** you use in your posts, it becomes dangerous if you start to lose sight of what's *really* important-- your customer.

This is about being whatever version of *you* that you need to be to attract the sort of people you want to attract.

And if that's too much pressure, then keep separate accounts for personal stuff and business stuff. *Lots of people do.* **No biggie.**

But ultimately, I love the challenge of thinking I have an important audience watching everything I do on social media.

> *It helps me keep things in perspective.*

> *It helps me see more humor in my everyday life.*

> *It helps me stay positive.*

Which is why lately, my news feed has become a bright and happy place full of kind, ambitious, generous people-- exactly the sorts of people I want around me in my life and in my business!

So if you want to attract confident, kind, positive people into your world? The first (and most effective) step is to **go out and be confident, kind and positive!**

That's the best way I know to put the "HOT" in *your perfectly imperfect* version of a hot mess.

Watch THIS

"What Introverts
and Soft Spoken
Entrepreneurs Need
to Know About
Personality Marketing"

thebookonpersonalitymarketing.com/video-4

• •

How to Use "Awesomeness By Association" to Position Yourself as an Expert

Have you ever heard the song "Hey, Ya" by Outkast? It was listed by Rolling Stone as *one of the greatest hits of ALL TIME.*

But you know what's crazy about that song?

When it first came out, *nobody liked it.*

The data didn't lie: when it came on the radio, everybody was switching stations. It sounded just a little bit *too different* from the other popular songs of that time.

You know what made it possible for that song nobody liked or noticed to become one of the greatest hits of all time?

Positioning.

The record execs behind Outkast made a point of making sure "Hey, Ya" got TONS of airplay, **positioned perfectly in between the songs that everybody knew and loved**-- so before long, we gave it a chance. Then it got stuck in our heads. *Then we loved it.*

That's what positioning does.

When I talk about the positioning strategy that I like to call "awesomeness by association", I simply mean putting something (or someone) who's relatively *unfamiliar* to us right next to something or someone who's relatively *familiar* to us, **who we already know and like.**

This is such a powerful strategy because it can help you, at least to some degree, shortcut the process of building credibility in your industry. If you can position yourself as *a peer to someone who's more well known than you are*, you can become associated with that person in a positive way.

Any feelings of trust that your prospect might have for this person can, *by your association with them,* **be transferred to you.**

A great example of this principle at work is podcaster Lewis Howes, who has played host to a star-studded roster of interviewees on his show, "The School of Greatness."

Although Lewis had plenty of his own personal successes to use in his positioning, *his association with some of the biggest names in entrepreneurship* have catapulted him to the forefront of his industry.

Interviewing influencers on a live show or podcast can also be a great way to grow your personal and professional network because *it benefits all parties involved*-- giving them **access to new people, more attention, more authority and more credibility.**

The concept of "awesomeness by association" explains why a great blog post can linger in obscurity forever on one blog, but when it gets published on a big popular blog, *it gets shared thousands of times.*

In today's content-saturated world, it's not always the best content that wins-- more often, it's the content that's published by the most well-known people.

Of course, there are two ways to handle this information: *you can complain about it, or you can use it to your advantage.*

Here's one example of the latter.

I saw an ad recently that made expert use of the "awesomeness by association" strategy. It was a life insurance company who teamed up with the popular blog, "Scary Mommy" to promote an article that had very little to do with life insurance, aside from one small mention.

In my opinion, it was a really well-executed campaign because *it took something patently un-sexy and boring* like life insurance and associated it with *something relevant and enjoyable* (like the playful, self-affirming content we've come to expect from Scary Mommy).

What campaigns like this teach us is that the specific *information* people have about us as brands can often be less important than the *feelings* they associate with us. Associating yourself with people, places or experiences that make your prospect feel *good* creates *good feelings around YOU* by association.

A couple of tips to get you started as you put this strategy to work in your business: **first, start small.** You'll get much farther much faster if you don't go after people with huge followings on day one-- (unless you already some sort of existing connection with them).

In any case, **it's going to be a lot easier to get on someone's radar if they're not getting tons messages from tons of people all the time.**

That said, if you really want to build relationships with big names in your industry, the best way to do it is either to:

> 1) hire them, **buy from them** or sign up for their programs,
> 2) go out of your way to **engage with them** in meaningful ways on social media, or

3) **learn about what they need** or care about and provide them with something valuable you know is going to knock their socks off.

And above all, **please be courteous** and ask yourself honestly, *what's in it for them, if they pay attention to you?*

How can you bring **remarkable amounts of value** to the table, rather than defaulting to the *"tit for tat", transactional* networking most people do?

When you build real relationships and deliver *real value,* people will naturally **want** to help you. They'll **want** to recommend you to their friends.

I can't tell you how often I hear of (*and experience firsthand!*) marketers pressuring entrepreneurs to share content in which they've been featured in a sort of **"I featured you so now you owe me access to your followers"** sort of spirit, and it's just *yucky.*

You can do better.

If you don't, chances are that your networking efforts won't take you *nearly* as far as they could have.

One more thing to consider on this subject before we wrap up-- awesomeness by association can also come from *associating yourself with positive outcomes* people might experience after using your product or service.

In other words, this particular sort of positioning doesn't always have to come from associating yourself with famous people. It can be even *better* to associate yourself with your own happy customers!

That's why whenever someone says something nice about my content or products, I make sure to take a screenshot so I can use it in one of my funnels.

Whenever I hear of a client getting positive results from our work together (and, happily, that happens quite often) I make a note of the specific results they achieved so I can **make sure their success gets properly celebrated!**

I've also seen people apply the principle of awesomeness by association by taking photos of themselves in beautiful settings and/or surrounded by beautiful things and then using those photos for their website and social media presence. This sort of visual statement can send a very powerful message about you as well.

Just do me a favor, won't you, and don't take a selfie in front of someone else's mansion or luxury car and claim it's yours! **You don't have to deceive people to prove you're cool. You ARE cool! I see that about you (or at least I assume it, because you're cool enough to be reading this)...**

...we just want to do what we can to make sure everybody else sees it, too.

The thing I love most about awesomeness by association as a strategy is that it (at least to some degree) *can level the playing field* for people who are just getting started-- **IF those beginners use it well**, of course...

So by now you probably get that in order to position yourself as an A-List industry leader, sometimes you need to focus on the outward stuff, but sometimes you also need to *turn inward and check in with yourself,* too...

• •

How "Knowing Your Type" Could Help You Sell More Stuff

I have a very vivid memory of the voice teacher I had in college. He was a short, chubby opera singer with a mustache who always wore a gold chain, and I absolutely loved taking lessons from him. **I feel like he really *got* me.**

In fact, in some ways he *got* me even a little bit more than I *got* myself.

One day during my lesson, he presented me with a new song he wanted to sing: "Stay With Me" from Into the Woods, sung by the character of the witch.

It's a great song, don't get me wrong, but as soon as I laid eyes on the sheet music I burst into tears.

He was SO confused.

"*Why* do you keep assigning me songs for *old women* and *ugly people?*"

See, I was still thinking I was going to grow up and be a Disney princess.

Except... **turns out, I'm not cut out for Disney princess-hood.**

And I had to come to terms with that.

After a solid 20 minutes of tears, he was finally able to convince me that this was actually a good thing-- that what we in showbiz call "character roles" *really are some of the best roles to play.*

Because here's the deal-- those "Disney Princess" types, as it turns out? *They're not all that memorable, and they're* **nowhere near as fun** *to watch.*

Now here's where this starts to get really cool for you: **you don't** *have* **to look amazing to market effectively with video.**

You just have to embrace your type.

We actors love to whine about "typecasting,", which is the word we use to describe what happens when directors make casting decisions *based on looks alone.*

But the fact of the matter is, everybody does it. We **do** make judgments based on looks, and by nature we're more likely to buy from people we find attractive-- so although it might be a tough conversation to have, it's important to think objectively about how to make the most of what you're working with... *aesthetically* speaking.

So here are three things you might want to consider when it comes to embracing your type:

1. It's Mostly About Confidence

The truth is, people of all shapes, sizes and colors have built HUGE personal brands based on their on-camera presence.

How is that possible?

Confidence, baby!

If you're dwelling on your insecurities about how you look or if you're trying to seem like someone you're not, *you're not going to be effective* on camera.

Confidence and charisma are HUGE, which is why when I work with clients I do everything I can to help them feel excited about their content strategy *by infusing it with their particular brand of nerdiness*-- I've always found that **that extra little boost in personality** can go a *long way* toward feeling comfortable on camera.

Think about some of your favorite comedic actors or musicians. A lot of them aren't "model-status-hot", right? But they're *super confident* and that's sexaaaay!

2. Lean In to Your "Different"

Colorful characters are the most memorable, so don't be afraid to stand out-- in fact, you might even want to embellish a little!

You can use your clothing, your hair, your makeup, the filter on your camera, even the backdrop behind you to say something about the unique character you want to create.

You want that image to be specific, interesting and clear.

> Michael Jackson wasn't just *your average* singer.
> Lucille Ball wasn't just *your average* tv personality.
> Donald Trump (no matter how you might feel about
> him) isn't just *your average* real estate mogul-turned-
> politician.

They (and many others) *leaned into what made them unique,* and
it certainly paid off for them!

But the question remains, *"exactly which of my unique traits
should I lean into? What sort of image should I be creating for
myself if I want to sell more stuff?"*

Here's the short answer...

3. Cast Yourself for the Customers You Want

Whatever you do, do NOT make the mistake of thinking you're
limited to marketing only to the people who will find you
physically attractive. *That is **not** the point here!*

The point is, you have to figure out who it is you're talking to,
and you have to become the version of yourself that stands to
appeal to that audience the most.

So if, for example, **you want to attract a really high-end
clientele, you might want to put some effort into making sure
your videos and your marketing assets in general have a high-
end look and feel.**

In one of my online courses, "Captivate On Camera", we talk
about a lot of things you can do to get that high-end look on a
budget, but here's what you need to know right now-- *this is not
about being phony.*

Whether we're aware of it or not, **we're all playing a part** or assuming a specific "character" based *who we believe ourselves to be.*

So if you're playing a role anyway, why not step into the role of the person your perfect customer wants you to be, or *at least* create the types of videos that your perfect customer wants to see?

If you're not doing that, you might not end up making as much money as you could have otherwise...

4. Like Attracts Like

Knowing that, you might then be wondering, *"how do I know who my perfect customer needs me to be?"*
Well, the easy answer to that question is to say that **like attracts like**. That's why a lot of married couples look alike.

So does that mean you can *only market* to people in your same demographic?

Not necessarily... but it might very well be effective for you, at least when you're getting started!

In my experience helping people make money from their personal brands, I almost always find that your most enthusiastic supporters are generally going to be **those who look, act and generally ARE *a lot like you!***

Now, that said, I don't want my fellow ad nerds out there going out and trying to target people with brown hair and blue eyes who are 5'4" and wear a size 8 shoe, because *1) you can't get that specific with your targeting*, and *2) you don't need to.*

But I think you'll find that putting your real self out there will attract more people like you. **It'll happen naturally.**

So why do I even bring it up, then?

Here's why.

Because **if you're flat broke and your life looks and feels like crap right now**, unless you make some changes to your mindset, whether you know it or not, you're going to be attracting people in that same position!

This is not pseudoscience. This is **pure psychology. This is a *fact.*** We want to be around people who make us feel good. Period.

So if you don't *feel good*, if you don't feel **confident** that you can deliver the outcome you're promising in your marketing, *that's something you've GOT to fix* if you want to be effective.

There are plenty of ways to do that.

> *You can work with a coach.*

> *You can work for free to build your confidence and expertise.*

> *You can entirely change the business you're in, if your heart isn't in it.*

There's no way I can know for sure what the answer might be for you.

But I *can* tell you this.

If you're creating videos, your videos MUST (at least in SOME ways-- not necessarily ALL the ways), *be aspirational* for the people who watch them, or it will be much more difficult create any sense of desire for the next step in your customer journey.

For now, let me circle back and drive this home one more time: *there's no reason for you to cry about your type like I did*, or wish you were someone else.

There is absolutely NOTHING WRONG with who you are. If you're smart about putting a positive spin on the "character" you create yourself to be, you don't have to be a picture perfect movie-star type.

In fact, it might even be a whole lot better if you're not.

In my case, I can tell you from experience that *being (and looking) a little weird and different* has been **incredibly helpful!**

It's what makes me memorable, and ***being memorable is AWESOME.***

So when we work together, *whenever that day comes*, here's what I want us to do: I want us to take the best of YOU and **pump up the volume on it**, bring out the most exciting, most compelling pieces of it and figure out how to turn those pieces into something meaningful for your ideal customers.
That's where your marketing starts to get really powerful.

But *you might have to do the tricky mindset work first*. You have to get out of your own head enough to **see how awesome you already are** and start embracing your type.

Even if you discover, like I did back in college, that your type is an old lady or a scary witch.

As it turns out, there's an audience for EVERY type, if you know how to speak to them effectively.

Which is exactly why you're reading this book, right?

Watch THIS

"7 Ways to Be Seen as an 'After' (Even If You Don't Feel Like One)"

thebookonpersonalitymarketing.com/video-5

I Have SO Many Different Interests and Skills... Which Should I Pursue?

Some people know exactly what they want to be when they "grow up".

Others want to be a BUNCH of different things.

And still others might have a preference among a handful of options regarding what career path to pursue, but **they're afraid of choosing the *wrong* path** and ending up broke and/or miserable.

If you can relate to any of that, this message is for you...

While there's no magical process for knowing *for sure* if you're on the right track before you test the waters, **there are some helpful items you might want to consider** as you make this kind of decision.

First, I want to speak to those of you who currently have several different career-related "plates spinning" at the same time. I think you *can* run more than one business successfully at a time, if that's something you want... *but...*

There are a couple of things that (in my opinion) need to be in place with the first business *before* it's a good idea to move on and build the second.

1. You need to have some sort of **marketing and sales system** and/or team in place that profitably generates leads and sales *for you* so that your business doesn't atrophy in your absence.
2. You need to make sure that **someone on your team can handle the administrative demands** (customer service, fulfillment, etc) of your first business if your second business demands more of your energy than you anticipated (which it probably will).

If you feel confident that those things are in place and that one business (or side of your business) *can run without you*, you're more than welcome to expand things as many times as you can successfully repeat this process.

Trying to pursue more than one of your interests at a time *can significantly decrease your ability to operate at maximum effectiveness* in either endeavor, so I generally recommend this "one passion at a time" approach-- UNLESS...

There is a way to pursue multiple interests by *combining* them, and in some cases **that only stands to increase your potential for success.**

I say that because often, *the most powerful way to "niche down" your message is to combine two distinct sides of what you have to offer.*

Let me give you an example.

I have a client who came to me with two very distinct passions and business ideas.

First, she wanted to **coach creative entrepreneurs** and help them become more confident.

Second, she has already developed a **unique hybrid of yoga and dance** and has been teaching it successfully for years.

Early on in our work together, it became abundantly clear that *combining those two passions* would not only make her work life much simpler, but it would also be a fantastic way to make her message stand out.

After all, *there are lots of people who want to coach entrepreneurs on confidence.*

There are a lot of yoga teachers with special methods.

But if we positioned **the combination of the two** as a groundbreaking new solution *with the express purpose* of using the mind/body connection to awaken new levels of confidence for overworked, stressed entrepreneurs... things could really start to get juicy, marketing-wise.

That's something you don't hear about every day.

It's not for everyone, BUT the people who it IS for will absolutely love it because they'll feel like it's *just for them*.

And that's a magical thing.

If you have the suspicion that your message or your market might be a little too broad to be effective, you might want to consider how it might look if you were to add another of your (relevant) passions to the mix.

It could be just the solution you're looking for.

But, for those of you who are stuck between several passions and you're pretty sure there's not a logical way to combine them, let's chat for a bit about some of the things you can think through as you prioritize *which passion to pursue first*.

This process is incredibly important, by the way, because while following one's passion is a powerful thing, *it doesn't always guarantee success*.

The following criteria will help you combine the wisdom of your head AND your heart to give you the best possible chance at success.

#1: Follow the Money

One thing we online marketing nerds don't talk about enough when we get on our soapboxes about the magical power of ads and sales funnels is this: *if your margins are too low, you might not be able to scale your business profitably--* **no matter *how* awesome your marketing message and ad strategy might be.**

If all you sell, for example, are $3 printables, unless your printables somehow go massively viral (which is unlikely), *you're going to have a tough time selling them at scale.*

I think it's really important to bring this up, because **advertising costs get higher and higher all the time** (*that's supply and demand for you*) so the harsh reality is that if your average customer is only worth about 7 bucks to you, your job might not be as simple as putting up a few sales pages and running some Facebook ads.

It's totally reasonable (*especially for a beginner*) to expect to spend $50-$100 **or even more** to get a new customer using paid advertising.

Of course, **it's absolutely possible to acquire customers for less**, but I just want to set some realistic expectations here. That number can vary a TON depending on what it is you sell and how effective your ads are.

Another way to think more practically about the earning potential of each of your interests is to ask yourself, "*Is there significant money being spent* on this sort of product/service in this particular industry?"

"*Do the people in this market spend the type of money I want to charge* on the type of solution I want to offer?"

As you ask questions like these, keep in mind that **competition, in this case, is a GOOD thing**. If other people or companies seem to be doing well selling similar things to what you'd like to sell, *that proves that there's a demand for it.*

Remember, there are SO MANY people in the world-- *there WILL BE room for you!*

That said...

#2: The riches are in the SUB-niches

I super-duper-really hope you know by now that the way to compete in ANY marketplace is to *set yourself apart* from your competitors.

That's why all of this "personality marketing" business is *so powerful*-- because **one of the easiest ways to unleash a brand's uniqueness is to tie it to one of the most unique creative sources in the whole wide world**-- *a living, breathing human being!*

But of course, that's only one small part of the process of differentiating a brand.

A lot of marketing teachers will tell you to *find your niche*-- find the unique group of people you will serve and the unique solution you'll offer them.

Fewer marketing teachers will tell you to take this process one step further and find a niche WITHIN that niche, or a *sub-niche*.

It might not always be necessary to do this, but it can be quite helpful in today's competitive landscape-- *especially* if you're not 100% clear why someone should buy from you as opposed to someone else like you.

So, considering the example I introduced before, in the case of my client, she could have stuck with just the one niche-- creative entrepreneurs. Choosing the SUB-niche, *creative entrepreneurs who have an interest in yoga*, gives her the opportunity to be a true pioneer in her space-- **maybe even THE go-to expert** for that small group of people.

Keep in mind, too, that a "small group of people" like this will still probably contain thousands (if not *hundreds of thousands*) of potential buyers!

So while some more scarcity-minded entrepreneurs might be concerned that they'll earn less by making their message this specific, savvy entrepreneurs know that *this sort of specificity stands to make them MORE money* and earn them MORE loyal customers than a broader, more all-inclusive message would.

#3: All you need is LOVE

It might seem obvious, but I'm gonna say it anyway: if your goal is to be a thought leader on a certain topic, *it should probably be a topic you want to talk about-- a LOT!*

Thought leadership, after all, is built on *content*.

And in most cases, **LOTS of content,** whether that takes the form of videos, podcast episodes, books, presentations, blog posts or any combination of those.

This means that *it could take months or even years* of producing these types of content for you to make a name for yourself, so you should probably choose a topic you'd be willing to spend a LOT of time thinking and talking about!

Which, of course, brings us back to the importance of nerdiness...

If you can't think of all that much to say about your chosen area of expertise, that might be a sign that your "nerdiness quotient" is insufficient to sustain your enthusiasm, which means you might need to reconsider the direction you're heading.

After all, entrepreneurship is hard, no matter WHAT you end up doing-- so you might as well choose to do something you find SUPER COOL!

#4: Do More of What Makes You Awesome

If you've gotten to this point and STILL don't feel clear about which of your passions to nurture first, consider this-- *do you have any special credibility or experience ALREADY* in any of your possible options that could help you get a bit of a head start?

When I say this, I mean--

Do you have any unique talents that have enabled you to accomplish impressive things in the past?

What experience do you have (work, hobbies, etc) that you could draw upon to establish your credibility as an expert?

Do you have any valuable skills that few others have?

Do you have any "claims to fame"-- things you've been recognized for, either by your peers or by an official organization?

Has any part of your life experience given you a unique perspective or ability to empathize with people who have a specific sort of problem or challenge?

These things could all be valuable, usable assets to help you establish yourself as a leader, even if you feel "brand new" in your space.

If you have something awesome in your toolbox already, you might as well put it to good use, right?

#5: Learn from your market

The moment my business and my brand began to really take off was the moment I decided to *adapt my message to match what I was hearing* over and over from my audience.

At the time, I was teaching the most valuable thing I knew how to teach *(how to build a business AND remain sane as a parent at the same time)* and it was moving along okay...

But as I talked to and engaged more and more with my audience, I kept hearing the same questions over and over: *"How do you make those videos? How do you come across so persuasively on camera?"*

That was a HUGE "a-ha" moment for me.

In fact, I can't believe I didn't think of it before.

Having come from a theatrical and creative writing background, it made SO MUCH SENSE to combine those things with my passion for marketing.

(Are you noticing the sub-niche here, by the way?)

It wasn't until I started to deliver *what my market was actually ASKING me to deliver* that I started to attract the kind of attention and income I'm blessed to enjoy today.

Market research is SUCH an important part of starting a business, and yet it's something that most entrepreneurs quickly gloss over *(if they do any at all).*

If you're smart enough to take the time to **learn as much as you can** about any market you want to enter, you'll collect a TON of valuable information.

You won't just learn about where you want to be, but you'll also start to notice the types of problems people really need solutions for, the specific words and phrases used in that market *(which you can later use in your marketing materials)*, **and the places where that market might feel under-served, where you might be able to really shine.**

NOTE: I want you to notice that I said to *"LEARN from your market."* I did *not* say that you should always *"LISTEN to your market"*-- sometimes, of course, you can and should, but if you followed every whim of what people told you, you might lose sight of the other valuable information you've collected as we've reviewed the previous four items.

Chew On THIS

Truth is, "the market" doesn't always know what it wants.

If you asked people how to price your services, for example, *they'd probably tell you to charge $5 for a service they might have been willing to pay $100 for*, **with the proper positioning.**

If you asked your cousin what you should do professionally, he or she would probably have *no idea what you're capable of*, having never worked with you in a professional setting.

Even if you ask around in a series of well-established groups of entrepreneurs on social media, the advice you get will most likely be varied-- **some of it will be great advice, *and some... not so much.***

So yes, *learn* from your market... but don't feel like you always have to *listen* to them.

Now, here's a little homework assignment for you. If you're still stuck trying to choose a direction for your business between a handful of options, I want you to spend a little time brainstorming through the items we just discussed, and I'll tell you what they are again so you have them all in one place, but this time I'll phrase them as questions so you can more easily think through your answers:

Do This NOW

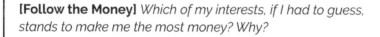

Write down your answers to the following questions:

[Follow the Money] *Which of my interests, if I had to guess, stands to make me the most money? Why?*

Do This NOW

(Continued)

[Riches in the Sub-Niches] *Would it make sense to combine two or even three of my interests to create a sub-niche to further differentiate myself from my competitors?*

[Passion and Perseverance] *What subject could I talk about for days? What do I like to read about, learn about, watch shows about? Could any of those interests connect in some way with one of the products or services I'd like to offer?*

[Credibility Assets] *What "credibility assets" do I currently have that I could use to set myself apart? Talents? Skills? Experience? Expertise? Unique Perspective?*

[Learn from your Market] *What sort of advice am I often asked for? When I post content on social media or on my blog, what sorts of material usually get the most engagement? Is there a need somewhere that I want to/feel qualified to fill, that isn't quite being filled just yet?*

Once you've worked through your answers to these questions, I'll issue you one more challenge-- trust your gut and *make a decision.*

In the end, you won't know for sure if you're moving in the right direction *until you try*, **so get to the trying part as soon as you can!** Keep in mind that making a decision now doesn't mean you have to stay committed to that decision forever.

Depending on how quickly you work, if you really commit to taking action, *you'll probably know sooner rather than later if your plan is working.* If it's not, **make adjustments until it does**. Eventually, you'll land on the right solution for you.

Chapter Six:

How to Design and Magnetize Your Dream Audience

Even If You Have a Special Gift for
Attracting Bottom Feeders
and Broke People
Right Now

The CRAZY-Powerful "First Step" Most Marketers Skip

Once you've got a handle on what your big idea is and you have a pretty good grasp on **how to position yourself as an expert** in that area, you'll want to find the group of people who's going to be most enthusiastic about that big idea *(and the most likely to pay you the money you want to be making)*.

And this is something very few marketers will tell you-- the customers you start with might not be the customers you end up with. This is really important to consider, especially in the beginning, because it's often a good idea to start by catering specifically to the people who are most likely to be your early adopters.

These are the people who want what you offer so much, who are in such urgent need of solutions to their problems that they're going to be a lot more patient with you as you work out the kinks in your business model.

They're also going to be more enthusiastic, more likely to share your stuff with their friends, and a lot more likely to buy.

Now, of course the question becomes, how do we find these people? Well, it begins with getting really specific about who you want to appeal to first.

Most of the business owners I've come across in my "marketing travels" are pretty single-minded when it comes to their strategies.

The thinking is pretty much always "what do I do if I wanna make money, NOW NOW NOW?"

And believe me, *I get it.*

That's marketing's job, after all, **to make you money.**

Of course you want that.

BUT -

You should also consider that moving slowly in the short term can sometimes be best for your bottom line in the long term.

This is particularly true for businesses who want to profitably sell their stuff via paid advertising, but who haven't yet laid the groundwork of building a warm audience.

A warm audience is a group of people who are already familiar with your brand and your message-- people who already, at least to some degree, know, like and trust you.

This is so important because unless we as consumers come across a product that's SO unique and remarkable and relevant that we just HAVE to have it immediately, we usually will need to come across your offer *on a few separate occasions* before we start to feel ready to hand over our hard-earned money to get it.

So when I hear that the biggest Facebook ad companies in the business are seeing a higher return on overall money invested when they run two campaigns instead of one (*in some cases spending twice as much so they can warm up the audience before putting a more aggressive sales message in front of them*), I can't say I'm surprised.

Always remember that **the goal, when you're advertising, is not to SAVE money-- it's to EARN money.**

And if building a warm audience first is a more reliable path to cash, then by all means, *that's exactly what we should be doing.*

Of course, if you're convinced of that by now, the question then becomes: *how do I go about building this "warm audience" you speak of?*

Well, **let's talk about that, shall we?**

In order to make the most of your warm audience once you have it, you need to have some sort of "bucket" in which to organize them so that you can get your marketing message in front of them again in the future, right?

So your first order of business should be to determine which "bucket" (or combination of buckets) you'd like to use to collect data about who these people are.

Each possible "bucket" has its own set of advantages and disadvantages, so we'll talk a little bit about what those might be so you can make a more educated decision about where you might like to start.

I'll organize the possible "buckets" your warm audience can fall into *in order of the necessary level of commitment to you and your brand.* In other words, at the top of the list will be the bucket that I think requires **the lowest level of commitment from the audience member**, and on down to **the highest level of commitment**.

The farther you go down the list, the more expensive these audience members will be to acquire, *but the more profitable they stand to be for you* in the long term.

Also, keep in mind that many members of your audience will fall into more than one of these groups, gradually moving through higher and higher levels of commitment IF you properly nurture them with quality content. That should be the goal.

1) Viewers/engagers

Today, especially if Facebook ads are part of your marketing strategy, you might want to consider using Facebook's ad platform to keep track of data regarding who has engaged with video or other content you've published on your business page.

Even if you don't do anything to set it up, Facebook is keeping track of who's engaging with your page, which is a really cool (and cost-effective) service they provide for us business owners in the hopes that one day we'll use that data to build more effective audiences for our ads.

The important thing to know about building your audience this way is that in order for Facebook to collect that data, you need to be publishing your content from a business page rather than a personal profile or a private group. If I go live, for example, on my personal profile, I can't show ads later to the people who tuned in to that. Facebook doesn't store that data for advertiser use, at least not right now (and I don't anticipate that they will in the future.)

Facebook doesn't actually want us doing business from personal accounts, anyway, so that's something you'll want to be careful about whether you plan on using ads or not.

2. Site Visitors

A step up from that sort of warm audience is **people who have visited your website**. I highly recommend that every website owner install at least a Facebook and Google tracking pixel on their site (if you don't know how to do that, a quick YouTube search can steer you in the right direction-- it's usually a simple "copy and paste" sort of setup, super simple.)

What these tracking pixels will allow you to do is **keep track of who's gone where on your website**, which can be incredibly powerful.

For those of you more advanced advertisers, you might already be aware that with pixels properly installed, you can pull interested prospects back *in at any stage of your sales process* with highly targeted, highly relevant ads to significantly increase the profitability of your ad strategy.

For example, if you wanted, you could get SO granular with your ads that if someone visits your checkout page but abandons their cart, you can set up your ad targeting to send a special message just to them *and even show them the very items they had in their cart!*

It's cool stuff, for sure.

3. Page followers

Next up on the "commitment scale" is people who liked (*and even better, followed*) your page or social media profile.

Keep in mind that the people who follow you won't always see your content; in many cases, you'll still need to pay to promote it.

But not always… ;) sometimes you get lucky.

Your job when people follow you on social media, as far as I'm concerned, is to make a killer first impression and hopefully use that unique moment of enthusiasm to move these new fans to the next level of commitment if at all possible.

When people first "like" my Facebook page, for example, I've pinned a post right there at the top that sends them straight over into my Facebook group-- which brings me to...

4. Group members

Whether it's on Facebook, LinkedIn or any other social network that allows for groups, you stand a better chance at having your content seen by your group members than by the people who just like or follow you.

That's why it pays to have a quality group.

I host mine on Facebook, and it's been a **huge source of new business** for me. Almost always, my clients join my group before they ever buy anything from me.

It makes sense, too, because when people are in your group, it gives them a chance to get to know you a little better-- to *spend some time in your little "world"* and see what you're all about so they can later determine if they'd like to be a customer.

However, this strategy only works if the content in your group is good!

It's SO RARE to come across a life-enhancing, value-driven group these days that when people see it, *they can't help but take notice.*

This should come as excellent news to you, of course, because I'm sure you're not planning on creating one of those spammy, sales-y, boring-sauce groups... right?

The logic here is simple. Share unto your group what you would like shared unto you.

Got it? Excellent. Moving on.

5. Messenger or text subscribers

Messenger bots are soooo hot right now-- little automated *"choose your own adventure" sorts of conversations* set up through Facebook messenger that allow you to build a whole new list of subscribers on a fun and interactive platform.

Some people are saying messenger bots will replace email...

I'm not so sure, only because social media etiquette should prevent us from sending Facebook messages anywhere near as often as we now send emails.

That's why I generally recommend **using a combination of both**, when you can.

The same sort of etiquette is also true for people who opt into your list to receive text messages. Where you can absolutely get away with sending 3, 5, in some cases even 7 emails a week, **people would never stand for that frequency via messenger or text** (*unless things have changed significantly since I wrote this book, which I'll admit is quite possible.*)

For a company like a restaurant or brick-and-mortar store, though, *these infrequent messages might be just the ticket* (since people don't generally want to receive tons of messages from places like those anyway.)

It really depends what business you're in, because of course there IS no "one size fits all" solution, *even (and maybe even ESPECIALLY) when it comes to personality marketing.*

As far as messenger bots are concerned, the place I feel they can be the most valuable is *deeper* **in your sales process**-- where people have shown some interest and you want to walk them through their options or some frequently asked questions, but you don't necessarily have the customer service team on hand to address the more common sorts of conversations that you know in advance that people might want to have.

Messenger bots can talk people through upsells and cross-sells too. You can even use them in print materials similarly to how you might use a QR code... *with a little creativity, the possibilities are endless!*

6. Freebie-seeker email subscribers

Now, it's getting even more fun! We are getting close to what most marketers consider the Holy Grail-- your email list. *Wheeee!*

For our purposes here, I want to make a distinction between two types of email subscribers: *freebie-seekers,* **and those who are** *highly engaged.*

Most people who opt in to your average list-building campaign will fall into the first camp, the "freebie seekers," *and that's okay.* That's just because in order to gain subscribers, most of us offer a freebie. If we didn't, if we just said "get on my email list for updates," we wouldn't get nearly as many subscribers. I'm hoping that's common knowledge by now.

If it's not, it should be! **Tell your friends!**

But as soon as people get on your email list, you have a new (and much more difficult) task to perform: you want to build the relationship with your subscribers to the point at which they move up to the next level of commitment...

7. Highly engaged email subscribers!

When your subscribers are highly engaged, they open your emails. They click through the links in your emails. And hopefully, one day, they *buy stuff* from you!

Where most marketers drop the ball is, they get a new email subscriber and think *"Yay! My job is done! Now I can send these people sales-y, value-less CRAP nuggets every two seconds!"*

Gross.

That's no way to build a relationship.

Once someone subscribes, your work is just beginning.

You want to make sure every email you send delivers value, whether or not someone ever clicks through to make a purchase from you. A highly engaged email subscriber?

That's where the money is, folks.

They'll gladly allow you into that most private inner sanctum, their email inbox, with your lovely and subtle sales messages, for years to come.

And that's a beautiful thing.

But it might not be *quite* as beautiful as...

8. Customers

The people who've bought from you once are considerably

more likely to buy from you again! *Woohoo!*

That means it's your job to continue to nurture those relationships-- to treat your buyers well. Not only does a high level of customer satisfaction give you *the best possible chance at repeat purchases*, it also puts you in a much better position to gain the next level of commitment...

9. Affiliates

Affiliates are SUPER-valuable, even if they don't have large audiences of their own, simply because it's more powerful to have *other people* talking about how awesome you are than it is to have *you* always out there talking about how awesome you are!

If your customers are willing to recommend you to their friends, with or without a commission, you'll be in excellent shape.

Are you starting to see the hierarchy?

*As you invest time, money and creativity into building a highly engaged and loyal audience, what you're really building is **an incredibly valuable asset that stands to make you lots and lots of money for years and years to come.***

The most important thing to remember, though, is that the power in your audience is only going to come when you build the right audience on the right message. You want your brand to be flexible enough that if you decide to pivot or change what you're offering slightly, *your audience will still stick with you.*

Do This | NOW

Write down your answers to the following questions:

Assess <u>what you're already doing to deepen the relationship with your audience</u> *at each level* so you can evaluate where you need to put more effort to amp up your levels of engagement (and, of course... *sales!*)

1) Viewers and Engagers

2) Site Visitors

3) Page Followers

4) Group Members

5) Messenger or text subscribers

Do This NOW

(Continued)

6) "Freebie seeker" email subscribers

7) Highly-engaged email subscribers

8) Customers

9) Affiliates

So of course, the question becomes, *how* do you go about building such an audience?

It all begins with deciding what sorts of content you'd like to share.

• •

Who Needs the Kardashians When We Have YOU?

Once you're ready to really start thinking of yourself as a media company, one of the first things you'll need to do is get clear about the content of your "show" (in other words, the content you'll be sharing online).

In order to get clear about that, let's think for a second-- **what does every great show have?**

- *Characters we like*
- *Believable, powerful performances*
- *Entertainment value/excitement/suspense/great storytelling*
- *A unique, clear premise or subject matter that we find interesting*

Those things are exactly what you're going to need in order to get results from your content, too.

NOTE; For the most part, we'll focus on video content here because I believe video to be the most emotionally compelling way to tell stories.

However, these same principles could **easily be applied to other content types** and still be effective (*hint: I'm using a lot of said principles right here in this book)!*

In any case, let's talk about the types of videos (or other content) your "show" will consist of.

As far as I'm concerned, videos that sell should always do one *or more* of the following things: **Educate, Demonstrate, Inspire or Entertain**.

Marketing videos that ***educate*** are all about making sure that your viewers *know what they need to know* before they'll be willing to buy from you.

These sorts of videos can **explain new concepts, answer questions,** or simply **open the viewer's eyes** to a problem they might not yet even know they have.

Marketing videos that ***demonstrate*** are the kind that actually *show you what it's like* to use and/or benefit from a product or service. These kinds of videos can be incredibly helpful because of a principle that pro salespeople like to call *"future pacing".*

Future pacing is a term that describes what happens when we enable the prospect to *envision in detail the experience or benefit they might enjoy* after they make the purchase.

One of the best ways to prove that you've got something awesome to offer is to **PROVE that it works,** rather than just talking about it, which is why demonstrations can be so effective.

Or, for example, if you were selling a special sort of skirt that fans out when you twirl around in a circle, it might be nice to actually *see it in action* so I could imagine what it might feel like to wear it.

I know that a video like that would certainly make the *"six year old aspiring Disney princess"* in ME pay attention.

That's the power of demonstration.

Marketing videos that ***inspire*** can be SUPER powerful because they're *1) really rare,* and *2) emotionally compelling.* If you can inspire someone to feel like **their life really will change for the better** as a result of becoming a customer, it's going to be a whole heck of alot easier to get them to make a purchase from you.

Of course, there are a variety of ways you can accomplish this. One commonly used way to inspire with video is to use underscoring-- **layering inspiring music into the background of the video** to convey the desired emotion.

Another way to inspire on camera is simply to *be inspired* yourself!

This is where a powerful, sincere on-camera performance

becomes so important, though, because **trying to fake this can most definitely work to your disadvantage**.

One of the best ways to inspire with video is to showcase the *results* of the use of your product or service-- show the viewer things like *happy customers* or *before and after photos* that prove how much better people's lives are after making this sort of purchase.

Finally, marketing videos that ***entertain*** can be really effective because, like inspiring videos, *they're much more likely to attract engagement* than your typical marketing video would.

A great way to make viewers more receptive to a marketing message is to **make it more entertaining**, whether that's using interesting visual imagery or incorporating humor or spectacle into your video concept.

If you're trying to be entertaining, though, just be sure to never lose sight of the fact that *a confused viewer does not buy*, so NEVER sacrifice the clarity of your message for the sake of entertainment.

Clarity should always come first.

I see this mistake being made in commercials all the time, by the way, and it drives me crazy! What's the point of making a commercial if when it's over, nobody even remembers what you were selling or why they should want it?

UGH.

LAME SAUCE, is what it is.

If you ever find yourself faced with the task of creating TV commercials (or any sort of video ad, for that matter...), *will you do me a favor?*

Please come and talk to me first.

Ridding the world of pointless commercials and lame-sauce video ads is a cause I hold *VERY near and dear to my heart.*

● ●

What should I create videos about, anyway?

If your offline marketing and selling success depends on building relationships, I would argue that **the same is true online as well**.

The only trouble is, we don't just "make friends with strangers" online like we do offline, when we're thrown into a social situation like a networking event or a community organization.

That's why the "rules of making friends" are somewhat different online-- **especially when you're on the road to making MASSIVE IMPACT and wanting to make those friends in a scalable way**.

Sure, you can go out and try to meet people in Facebook groups and such, but if you want a "friend making strategy" that will NOT be limited by the amount of free time you have available every day, as far as I know you really only have one option: *to create content that's so awesome, **people want to follow you for more.***

When I'm brainstorming content ideas, I like to make a big list of the **problems or questions** I know my ideal customer is likely to have before buying my product or service.

I put those all in what I like to call my "idea bank" because each one could be its own stand-alone video.

Something else you should put in your idea bank (*which you should keep somewhere you can access it easily*) are any stories from your life, your clients' lives or just the world around you that you could use to **illustrate some small piece of your message** or further *inspire your viewers to take the next step* with you.

Lately, this has become such a habit for me that I see ideas for videos popping up all around me, almost every single day. It's about **keeping your eyes open to the lessons around you**, and then finding a way to work them into your sales message.

Stories, by the way, are what make it *impossible* for you to ever run out of ideas for things you could make videos about-- because **you can only give the same sales pitch once or twice** *before people get sick of it*, but people will listen to great stories all day long-- *even if they all point to the same conclusion.*

The way to integrate this kind of storytelling into your script is to practice what I call the "from me to you" transition every time you use story.

This is really simple.

All you have to do is tell a story that means something to you, then explain what it means for them.

If you don't finish up your story by making it clear what it could or should mean to your viewer, the impact of that story is likely to fall on deaf ears. *You really do have to spell it out for people.*

The reason this is so powerful, of course, is because the more these viewers can **see themselves in your story**, the more they're going to trust that *you're the perfect person to get them where they want to go.*

With that in mind...

As you map out your content calendar, ask yourself this:

Where DOES my "perfect person" want to go?

What content could I create for them that would give me the best shot at proving to them that I can get them there?

If you have a clear, unique, compelling answer to those questions, you're well on your way to a DYNAMITE personality marketing strategy.

The key to mastering this sort of strategy is to ***really think*** about **the specific benefit your content will provide** to your audience, or in other words, *why they should pay attention* in the first place.

In order to help you find that clarity, let's talk about some of the steps I often walk through with my clients to help *them* clarify this stuff, so they can **send a compelling and sales-friendly message** *every time* they hit "publish."

• •

The Three Elements of an A-List Content Strategy

Three elements you can use help your content stand out (AND sell stuff) are:

> **1) your "big idea"**
> **2) your "hook", and**
> **3) your primary pitch**

We'll talk through each of those elements in a second, but first I want to give you a little bit of time to think through the content topic brainstorming process, as it might help you make sense of what's coming...

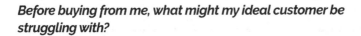

Do This NOW

Write down your answers to the following questions:

Before buying from me, what might my ideal customer be struggling with?

AFTER buying from me, what new experiences or feelings might my ideal customer be able to enjoy?

What problems could I solve in my content that might otherwise prevent my ideal customer from buying from me?

What questions could I answer that would eliminate any possible confusion my ideal customer might have about why they should buy from me?

What stories could I tell that might enable me to illustrate to my ideal customer an example of how what I'm offering could change their current situation?

What's the big idea?

Let's talk for a bit now about your "big idea" and where it fits into your marketing strategy.

We've touched on this already, but the time has come to get even more specific about **how to get it right** *from day one.* Again, the easiest parallel for me to draw regarding your big idea is to talk about it as if you're creating a reality show (*which, in a lot of ways, you are*). In that sense, your "big idea" would be the **topic or subject matter** of your show. *What it's about*, in general.

So let's use one of my favorite shows, Fixer Upper, as an example. Their "big idea" (or *the subject* of their show) is that they're going to take old homes and "fix them up" beautifully for their clients. That's it. **Super simple, even a little bit general**-- *but that's okay*, because it then gets more specific and unique from there once we combine the big idea with the hook.

And once again: **if you think your big idea is a product, you haven't found it yet.**

At least, not if you're committed to a relationship-based content marketing strategy.

Think about it:

People rarely watch shows that are *just* about products-- well, *on occasion* we might watch an infomercial, but we won't tune in to the same infomercial *over and over for years*.

Transactional, "buy this 'cause it's on sale today" marketing like that *doesn't create a lasting relationship*. **There's no loyalty being built there.**

And even worse, the *less* your unique contribution is needed to facilitate that transaction, the *easier it is to replace you* with technology.

I bring this up because more and more, people who act as the "middleman" in the sales process (*think realtors, insurance agents, ecommerce store owners and more*) are raising concerns about their roles being replaced by software platforms, apps and major online platforms like Amazon.

Their concern is, *if tomorrow's buyers really can buy what I sell* ***without my help...*** *what happens to my career?*

The good news is, there are still *lots of people* who still *prefer to do business with **real humans***, and more still who *prefer to **buy from real humans who also happen to be great salespeople!***

A great salesperson is one who knows that ***serving* is the key to selling.**

So online, *our content* is the way we serve. *It's the way we show we care.*

But if the people who come across your content can't **very easily tell** what it's all about or *what's in it for them?*

Your efforts will have been, in large part, wasted.

You'll know you've landed on your content's big idea when you can describe in one short sentence or phrase:

- **the type of problem you're going to solve**
- **the type of question you're going to answer**
- **the type of information you're going to share**
- **and/or the specific form of entertainment you're going to provide.**

It can come in a lot of different forms, but it is crucial to be clear on this, because **the consistency of this theme** is what's going to teach your viewer, "*if I come back for more of these videos, I know what to expect.*"

See, where most business owners miss out is they focus all of their content on their products and services, and **there's only so much of that kind of content that people can take**. But if your content is about a *lifestyle* and your products and services are just *one of many ways that you show up to enrich and support that lifestyle*, it's going to be **a lot more attractive** to potential customers.

Why?

Because *nobody wants to be sold to all the time.*

We're quite guarded about the sales messages we'll allow into our world (*and quite skeptical, even about those that we **do** allow in*) so you've got to figure out **how to make your content so attractive** and so value-driven that it *proves* to them that you *really do want to help them, rather than just take their money and skip away, saying* **"Muahahaaaaa!** *So long, SUCKER!!!"*

If your content *really is* made for your customers' benefit as well as your own, prospects will be happy to engage with it **often and for a long time to come**, as opposed to getting *burned out and annoyed* by hearing you offer them the same thing, over and over, day in and day out.

Need some help figuring out what your big idea will be?

Here's one trick you could try:

If you take a look at the cross-section of all the things you want to do, offer or teach, you're probably going to notice some **common themes that tie them all together.**

For bonus points, center your content around a big idea that has to do with a juicy, relevant *benefit* that your product or service also provides.

In my case, I've worked hard to establish that my big idea hinges on the simple outcome of *selling more stuff*-- because not only is that outcome relevant to **several distinct things I geek out about** all the time, it's also relevant to **every product and service I have to offer** my audience.

Under the "sell more stuff" umbrella, there are *tons* of content possibilities. I can talk about ads, sales conversations, email, mindset, communication skills, behavioral psychology... **so long as it ties back to selling more stuff**, I can geek out with you guys about ALL of it!

So many of you come to me with questions about how to sell

more stuff *without* annoying people or "being too sales-y", but I have a **really fun secret** to share with you:

The great thing about finding your "big idea" is that when it's harmonious with the various things you offer, *you CAN always be selling* because you'll be practicing **the "by the way" principle**-- pulling them in with great content, and then seamlessly moving into saying "by the way, if you REALLY want to step into this lifestyle, here's how I can help."

It never has to feel sales-y because it's just a natural extension of the **value you're already providing.**

And that's not the *only* cool thing about this strategy...

Zeroing in on your "big idea" is the only way I know that you can keep a consistent brand for years to come, **even if your business changes directions** or you offer something different, **your audience is still going to be valuable and relevant** because they're likely to be interested in just about anything you might offer because it's all part of that lifestyle or that Big Idea.

Here's why a content-focused (*rather than a product-focused*) big idea is so much cooler-- because assuming your content is engaging and heartfelt and enthusiastic, your customer will willingly and frequently connect with **the most compelling emotional reason to buy from you**-- the thing they *really* want-- the *feeling* they really want to feel.

● ●

The Hook Brings You Back

The second thing we need to get clear on is what your "hook" is-- because remember, we're using content to basically create a mini-version of a reality show.

So your big idea is going to play into the hook, for sure, but **we also need to think about what makes you and/or your product or service interesting**-- we need to *think about this like a TV* *producer would* and make sure we do everything we can to make your content enjoyable to watch.

So if your big idea is "the ice cream in the sundae", your hook acts like the toppings-- *gives it that little extra uniqueness and flair* that makes it really memorable.

Can you create great content without a hook? **Certainly**. And you might not know right away what your hook should be, either.

That's okay too. **Don't let that stop you** from getting out there and *creating*. You can always discover new possibilities and add in more fun nuances later, as you go.

Sometimes I'll be working with someone for two months and suddenly at the grocery store I'll have a massive epiphany about something brilliant they could do in their marketing.

More often, *they* have epiphanies like that.

It's tough to force the process, so *don't feel like you need to rush it.*

That said, **if you really want to figure this part out now**, going through this brainstorming process can help you take it to the next level.

Do This **NOW**

Look over this list of brainstorming questions to get your creative juices flowing. Then make some notes if any fun ideas occur to you regarding your hook.

What **quirks** do you have that you can take advantage of?

What assets do you have that could make your videos stand out from other videos? **For instance...**

Do you have a really cool-looking room where you could shoot?

Do you have, like, 149 different scarves you could rotate through?

Are you hilarious? Grumpy? Crass? Old-fashioned? Trendy?

Could you make jokes about the thing you sell?

Could you sing about it? Dance while using it? Make things with it?

Is life at your house *unconventional or crazy* in a way that some people might find fascinating?

This list is *by no means* exhaustive.

What I'm getting at here is, once you know your subject matter, it can be really helpful to **layer some elements of entertainment value** on top of that. That's what's going to enable you to *catch people's attention* and then hopefully *keep their attention* long term, because your content will be memorable and engaging.

Might you turn people off with your quirkiness?

It's possible.

And that's okay.

Because it's often lot more effective to be memorable *and* off-putting to some people than it is to try to please everyone, dilute your message and make mediocre videos no one's going to remember.

So *lean in* to the quirky stuff that makes you YOU.

Let your nerd flag fly.

Just remember, this is not about becoming someone you're not. It's not about acting like a *weirdo* just to get attention.

It's similar to the way a caricature artist would draw a caricature of you-- they do it by **taking your most interesting features** and then *exaggerating them* to make your portrait look a little more fun and unique-- but **they're still *your* features.**

Do you see the distinction?

In order to discover the subtle nuances of your "hook", simply **look for what's already there,** *find the most interesting parts*, and think about ways you could amplify or call attention to them to add a touch more entertainment value to your content.

For example, if you trip over your words a lot when you're filming, maybe you could add bloopers or outtakes.

If you get really mad about things, maybe you could take everyday video topics and turn them into rants.

If your house is always a mess, maybe you could film "from the trenches" and always shoot from in the midst of the mess, like sticking your face out from under a pile of clothes.

There are endless possibilities, but the key is to **keep it authentic to you**, keep it consistent and above all, keep it interesting.

● ●

"Sharing Fun Content Is Lovely... but How Do I Actually SELL Stuff?"

In order for your content to produce actual *sales*, it's going to need to lead your audience somewhere. While you might eventually have several different possible offers and/or funnels to promote, it's simplest to begin with one **"primary pitch"**.

This is going to be different from your big idea because remember, your big idea is all about the content you'll be sharing organically to build your audience. That content can (and should) **lead *into* your pitch**, or into the next step in your sales funnel.

Most commonly, you'll be pitching **some sort of entry-level offer** you can mention at the end of your videos to get your viewer's contact information, thus enabling you to take the relationship that one step closer to the sale.

What should the next step, entry-level offer or "primary pitch" look like?

Well, that's up to you.

The best place to start is to think about what the next logical step in the customer relationship might need to be, once someone takes an interest in what you have to say.

> *What's the first thing they should know about you, your process or your product?*

> *What's the first thing they need to experience in order to begin developing* **the level of belief they'll need** *before they're willing to buy?*

> *What sort of contact information is* **most important for you to get** *from them in order for you to initiate your follow-up and nurturing plans? (***Hint: the most commonly gathered information for this sort of offer is an email address...*** *that may or may not change in the future...)*

> *What* **problem** *do they have that would be worth sharing that information with you to solve?*

> *What* **specific result** *would they be willing to share that information in order to accomplish?*

The reason it's so important to get this right is that *this offer will serve as one of most prominent pieces of "bait" you'll be using to "reel in" your perfect customer.*

Over and over again, when I work with clients, I see them *putting* **the wrong bait** *in front of people and wondering why they don't buy*, when it's quite possible that the thing they're offering to initiate the sales conversation could be attracting the wrong audience in the first place.

But we'll get more into those sorts of details in the next chapter...

Do This NOW

Step 1: Write down a list of ideas for each category of your strategy.
Step 2: Circle the best idea in each category.
Step 3: Assess to make sure all the circled items work together perfectly!

Big Idea (The general, over-arching topic for your "show" or your content as a whole)

Hook (The more specific details that make your content more memorable, distinct and engaging)

Primary Pitch (The thing you *most want your customer to do* after they engage with your content for the first time, or the first logical step for them to take "into your world"-- not to worry, we'll discuss this further in the next chapter if you're stumped right now**)**

Chapter Seven:
How to Magically, Automatically and Profitably Turn Content Into Cash Flow

(Fancy Funnel Tech Wizardry Optional)

Yeah, Baby!

So! Now you've got your big idea, your enthusiastic audience and your "essence of after-ness", that positioning that tells people you're 100% legit (perhaps even too legit to quit, if you will).

You've thought through the subject matter of your online "show" and even dreamed up some *killer content ideas* that are **perfectly suited** to set you up for sales success.

Right?

Excellent! **Good for you!**

Next *(because you're reading this, which means you are interested in marketing like the a-listers in your industry do...)* we're going to want to incorporate some sort of automation into your sales process to **make sure it's scalable.**

If we don't do that, you can still create a successful business-- *just be aware that you'll need to create it one relationship and one conversation at a time,* **which can take quite a bit longer.**

That sort of growth strategy is not primarily what I like to teach, mostly just because *non-scalable growth strategies make me feel oddly claustrophobic...*

However, I often recommend that my clients start out there-- having *as many conversations as they possibly can,* for the sake of cultivating a deeper understanding of their customers' needs, questions, fears and desires.

But there comes a time in most every aspiring game-changer's career when they start to crave something a little more... *shall we say,* **world domination friendly?**

If automation and scalability are what you're after, then *a sales funnel* is most likely what you'll need.

If you're unfamiliar with the term "sales funnel", you might have heard it referred to as a "customer journey," a "sales pipeline" or an "online marketing machine."

Or maybe something different. Or maybe none of the above.

Whatever you want to call it, it's essentially the same-- the goal being to **put a little money into advertising and get a whole bunch more money out** by strategically automating the process of turning a prospect into a customer.

A sales funnel enables us to do that by automatically sending the prospect through a series of steps that tell them what they need to know about what we have to offer so that eventually (*hopefully!*) **they end up *buying things!***

Maybe even *a LOT of things!*

The ads, sales pages, emails, follow up messages, order pages and other marketing assets we use to make this process happen online (*with the help of, in some more advanced cases, some offline nurturing as well*) are the pieces that make up the sales funnel.

Chew On THIS

Funnels can range from very
simple to very complicated

Ad
▼
Order Page
▼
Thank You Page

Ad
▼
Retargeting Campaign
▼
Opt In Page
▼
Thank You Page Upsell with Order Form Bump
▼
One Time Offer
▼
Downsell
▼
Cross-sell
▼
Follow Up Sequence
▼
Text Reminder
▼
Webinar
▼
Questionnaire
▼
Call
▼
Sale
▼
Upsell
▼
Etc, Etc, Etc

What I will NOT recommend is that you try to make things too complicated too soon, like I did, before you've first had some time to experiment with a much simpler version of your funnel. **You can always add more bells and whistles and steps** later if you want to, but you might find that you don't need to at all-- it really just depends on what you sell.

The biggest mistake you could make as far as the funnel stuff goes is to *assume you don't need one*; that it's not relevant to your business.

If there are things you often say, questions you often answer, products you often sell in a certain order, objections you often encounter or demonstrations you often give during your sales process, you could probably benefit greatly from incorporating them into a sales funnel.

I've yet to come across a type of business that couldn't benefit from at least a *little bit* of funnel-ness to get things moving and make things more efficient.

Automating at least *some* of your sales process will free up your time and resources and enable you to do more of what you do best.

Remember-- you can have the most magnetic personal brand in the world and the snazziest videos ever, but *if you don't have the foundations of a solid business behind it*, it's not going to matter all that much.

That said, *there's no need to be intimidated.*

Building that automated moneymaking foundation doesn't have to be complicated. We can start by automating one or two things and then grow from there.

You could automate and "**funnel-ize**" some (if not all) of...

- Your lead generation
- Your lead nurturing

- Your appointment scheduling
- Your lead qualification
- Your pre-call positioning
- Your conversion tracking
- Your sales presentation
- Your recruitment process
- Your hiring process
- Your sales call follow-up
- Your referral and testimonial requests
- Your follow-up offers
- Your special promotions
- ...and more!

I'll just offer you one quick caution-- some entrepreneurs (*ahem... like ME*) get so excited about hopping on the "automation train" that they make the mistake of **over-automating** things that really would benefit from a more human touch.

So be cautious about relying too heavily on technology, tools and templates-- *especially* when it comes to anything customer-facing, and always make sure to test and keep an eye on whatever you automate to make sure it still has that all-important **personality** that makes everything *work*.

• •

The Losing Battle of Chasing Unicorns

I'll admit it.

Depending on what you sell-- **if it's unique enough and the value is clear enough**-- IT IS POSSIBLE for a "love at first sight" sort of scenario in which someone will click through and buy *without any previous knowledge of you* or your product.

However, if your marketing strategy depends on **magical unicorn prospects** such as those, you'd better have a *really cool/unique product* with some *serious margins and/or customer value optimization* working for you, because otherwise you might be in pretty big trouble.

A sales funnel isn't *just* about generating sales. It's about creating rapport and trust and ideally, **fans for life.**

If you're not careful, you could be committing the grave error of creating what I like to call *"lazy jerkface" marketing*-- acting like that obnoxious dude at a party who's like, "Nice to meet you. Let's talk about me!"

"Lazy jerkface" marketing often takes the form of **"product-first" marketing**-- in other words, doing nothing more than putting a picture of a product in front of a stranger and saying "buy this now!"

And while it can be tempting to try that, *it's rarely the best option* to do so.

In most cases, it's wasteful to go for the sale right away because you don't give these people the option to get to know you *(let alone experience your product or brand)* and unless you have a ginormous ad budget, you're not going to get in front of them *frequently enough* to stay top of mind **so that they remember you when the time comes that they ARE ready** for what you're offering.

Sure, you can go straight for the sale on Google and sometimes on more visually-oriented platforms like Pinterest or Instagram... maybe even Facebook. **It might make sense, depending on what you sell.**

However, I want to *seriously stress* a couple of the major flaws that might accompany a strategy like this in the hopes that you eager beavers will proceed with caution:

1. It can be lot harder to create a *long-standing relationship with your customer* when you're taking this sort of "product first" approach. Sure, you might see some short term results, but long term **you might not be able to build a sustainable business on the lifetime value of**

your customers since they fall more into the "*impulse buyer*" category than they will the "*true fan/devoted advocate*" category.

2. Most likely, the majority of individuals who see your offer *won't want or need what you're offering right that second*, but they **might** be in a buying mood later. That's why it might be a mistake to go for the sale right away-- **if you don't capture their information and do what it takes to stay on their radar until they *are* ready to buy, they will have long since forgotten you by then.**

That's why I most often advocate using social media ads to **build your email list and/or your warm audience** as opposed to directly selling-- because that way, you can generate leads *and nurture them over time*, capturing a much bigger portion of the pool of potential buyers who you would have totally missed out on otherwise.

Designing your Minimum Viable Marketing Plan (the simple version of your plan, *the one you can execute on well using the time and resources you currently have*) begins with a solid understanding of the "conversation" that needs to be had between your prospect and your brand **in order to generate a loyal, enthusiastic customer relationship.**

How do you map out that "conversation" and use automation to help you have it online?

You can start by figuring out the *primary problem* someone might experience, or possibly a *desire* or *question* they might have that might show that they're the type of person who's most likely to buy your stuff.

Once you're clear on that, you'll want to carefully craft some sort of free content or a low-ticket product to offer them that will *address* that problem, desire or question.

At that point we'll use pay-per-click ads to drive targeted traffic to a landing page where we'll offer that "value nugget" in exchange for the prospect's contact information. We'll then use that contact information to *send more marketing messages* to that prospect until they ask us to stop.

Which, hopefully they **never will** *because the messages we send them will be* **that awesome!**

The reason I love building "minimum viable marketing funnels" is because they make it possible to very quickly answer one simple question:

"Are we or are we not offering something people will buy?"

And/or...

"If this IS something people are buying from other people, am I talking about it in a way that makes them want to get it from ME?"

I mean, aren't those some of *the most important questions you can ask* about your stuff?

If the answer is "Yes, they will buy it," then you should know that fairly quickly.

The next step is to **optimize things** so we can cut your costs down as low as possible and increase your customer value so they buy even more from you.

If the answer is, "No, they're not buying," that's fine too, it just means we need to **keep tweaking things** like the words we use, the sequence of the offers, the structure of the pages and so on until we can turn that around.

During this phase, the goal is to *get everything fully functioning and profitable* so that later, when we go to build buzz and grow your following and get you on TV and speaking and writing books, we actually have a **solid, scalable customer journey** ready and waiting on the back end.

That way we don't spend the next five years building a following around something that was never going to make money in the first place.

'Cause that does NOT sound awesome.

• •

Finding the Right "Bait"

As we talked about before, *this is an absolutely CRUCIAL step* because **the results of your marketing depend**, in large part, on **the audience you attract.**

For example, if your ad message attracts **those who have only a casual interest in your field of expertise** but your ultimate offer requires a *burning desire* to solve a specific problem, you might run into some conversion issues when it comes time to make an offer.

That's why one of the best places to start when designing your funnel is to **zero in on "symptoms"**-- specific issues being faced by your customer and your customer alone.

One of the ad campaigns I've run recently, for example, is a content video I'm promoting that addresses a *worry I hear from some of my best prospects* all the time:

"How do I avoid the dreaded "Facebook ad flop" (aka-- that very depressing moment when I find that my ad spend just went down the drain)?"

In order to make sure I'm attracting the proper audience with this video, though, **I don't stop there.** I've pinpointed a few *key characteristics* of my ideal customer that I want this ad to speak to, so both *in the written copy of the ad AND the ad video script*, I make it clear:

1. That this message is for **people whose businesses rely on their personal brand**
2. That it's for **people who want to scale their potential for**

impact with paid advertising

3. That they're (at least to some degree) **interested in video ads and channeling their inner "nerd,"** as we've discussed here.

The reason I've sent that ad out "on the front lines" of my marketing is because I know that later on, when I put subsequent offers and ads in front of that same audience, *my marketing dollars will much less likely to go to waste* because **my audience will have been carefully and automatically isolated and vetted** by their interest in my "bait".

That said, if you're not ready to get nerdy with a multi-tiered retargeting campaign just yet, you could also think of your "bait" as we discussed it previously-- as **the free piece of content you offer prospects in exchange for their contact information.**

This is commonly called a *"lead magnet"*, a *"freemium"* or a *"freebie."*

Here are some examples of commonly used lead magnets:

- Checklists
- Cheat sheets
- Resource guides
- Video tutorials
- Webinars
- Quizzes
- Challenges
- Video series-es ;)

Keep in mind that **the best way to choose the topic and title for your lead magnet is to be strategic about the *pain point* it addresses**-- because in many cases, *the most important characteristic of the audience you build will be the pain or concern they're experiencing* when they find you.

What are some key characteristics that YOU might want to call out as you build YOUR ideal audience?

• •

Serving the Proper Appetizer

Once you're clear on what the right bait should be to draw out your perfect audience, your first order of business should be to **give your audience members the opportunity to experience whatever they might need to experience** *to become "a believer" in your product, your service and/or you.*

The way to do that is to use the first step in your funnel to **give your prospect the perfect "taste" of your product or service** that's *most likely to leave them wanting more.*

That might mean offering them a *low-cost product, a sample,* or just *a **great experience** with the free content they'll get for signing up to get your lead magnet.* There's no "perfect way" to do this, so I won't dwell on the tactical options right now, except to say that your goal should be to provide **something awesome** right off the bat that leaves a great first impression *while still* leaving the prospect wanting more.

Personally, most of my highest-performing ad campaigns and funnels are those in which I send my video viewers (*who find my videos and ads via both paid AND free traffic*) to what I call a "**primary selling video**".

"Primary Selling Video" (PSV) is the term I use to describe whatever sort of video content you might want to use (whether that's a **webinar, a masterclass or a video series**) to make your main offer.

You might end up with more than one of these, by the way.

Think about it like this -- anything you sell that requires some sort of **demonstration, conversation or presentation** could also be sold with a PSV.

For your PSV, our goal is to make it appear *compelling and special enough that your viewer would want to give you their email address (and maybe even MORE information)* in order to watch it.

That's the goal here-- preparing some sort of sales-oriented video content that also provides value to the viewer *whether or not they buy* from you.

Whether or not you're ready to spend money using ads to send people to your PSV, you can still drive traffic to it *via the content videos you're already sharing*.

At the end of each of your regular content videos (or what I call your "**secondary selling videos**") you can then say something like, *"If you want to know more about XYZ, make sure to sign up to get my free training, [TITLE OF FREE TRAINING]."*

Another way to think about what this "primary selling video" should be about, or what your "primary pitch" should be is to think about *the most compelling story you could tell, problem you could solve or question you could answer* that might logically lead this person to do the thing you most want them to do.

It's absolutely *imperative* that you figure out a powerful topic and headline for your PSV because it's such a pivotal piece of your sales process. Remember, it has to be powerful, engaging and attractive enough *that your ideal customer won't just **sign up to see it***, but also that they'll *stick around to watch it **and eventually take the NEXT step*** at the end.

It's a subtle art and science, figuring out **how much to give away** and **how much to hold back**, but *assuming you can hold your prospect's attention*, the next element you'll want to incorporate into your funnel should be...

● ●

Anticipating the Obstacles

A lot of marketers run into trouble with their sales because **they're over-teaching and under-selling.**

The danger with giving your prospect too much information is that **rather than *empowering* them** to take the next (and, in my opinion, most powerful) step in the growth process *by making a purchase*, what you're actually doing is ***overwhelming* them.**

That's why an effective, content-based marketing strategy actually has more to do with ***overcoming obstacles to the sale*** than it has to do with *sharing every last thing there is to know* about your area of expertise just to prove your worthiness.

As you design the content you'll use to facilitate this stage of the sales process, you'll want to think in terms of **creating the content so that it will anticipate and address common questions and concerns** *that might stand between the prospect and the decision to purchase* what you want them to purchase, or do what you want them to do.

● ●

Taking It to the Next Level

Depending on what it is that you sell, at some point or another you might want to consider **adding more steps to your sales funnel** to increase the lifetime value of your customers, thereby *enabling you to spend more to acquire them* (which is essential to your ability to scale up your marketing presence)!

Typically, this is done by **luring your prospects back into your funnel** repeatedly over time *by offering them more awesome content*, so that you can then *offer them more products and services* as the relationship deepens (which, of course, **it should**, so long as you continue to nurture it with high-quality content).

It is also often done by placing several different offers in a logical sequence, one right after the other, **during the checkout process**. This is a largely underutilized and *massively powerful tactic* for making the most of the buyer momentum that peaks at the point of sale.

These additional offers could take the form of:

- **Upsells** (something you offer that is more expensive than the product the customer bought previously-- usually something that would add a separate component of value that would take their experience to the next level)
- **Downsells** (something less expensive, but related to the offer you just made-- many marketers offer these if/when the prospect elects NOT to buy something)
- **Cross-sells** (something complementary to what you've just sold that could further enhance their result or experience)
- **Affiliate offers** (products sold by other companies that might also be relevant to your customer-- if they have affiliate programs, you could earn a commission for each sale)
- **Affiliate relationships** (in which your customer believes in your product SO much, they will share it with their network FOR YOU in exchange for commissions)

There are a lot of ways to increase the value of the leads you're bringing in, whether you make your offers *right away* or *months or even years into the future*. To explain each option could probably fill another book entirely.

For now, I'll leave you with this: **never assume that your sales cycle is a "one shot" deal.** After all, *why use personality marketing at all* if your intention isn't to build a lasting and profitable relationship?

If you launch an ad campaign and don't break even right away, remember this-- **all is *not* lost!**

If your ad and funnel strategy are sound and you're committed to nurturing your leads with a consistent supply of quality content over time, **you'll still have plenty of opportunities to create a return on the money you're investing** once these prospects have some time to get to know you better.

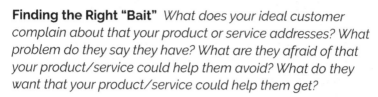

Do This NOW

Write down your answers to the following questions:

Finding the Right "Bait" *What does your ideal customer complain about that your product or service addresses? What problem do they say they have? What are they afraid of that your product/service could help them avoid? What do they want that your product/service could help them get?*

Serving the Proper Appetizer *What is the first thing your customers usually buy from you or want to learn from you that might open the door to wanting more?*

Anticipating the Obstacles *What questions do your prospects need answered before they're typically ready to buy? How would you answer them? What objections tend to come up during the sales process?*

Taking it to the Next Level *What needs to happen in order to make a compelling case for your additional products and services? Do you need to have a conversation? If so, what needs to be established prior to that conversation so that the prospect will be ready? How do you create or amplify the desire for more?*

A Few Fun Specifics for Your Sales Scripting Enjoyment

Every time I go to write a video script for something I'd like to share with my audience, I begin with the same basic template, which looks like this:

1. **Problem/Callout**
2. **Teaser**
3. **Content**
4. **Teaser**
5. **Call-to-action**

Let's break that down.

In the beginning of my video, I want to introduce what we're going to talk about, but I want to introduce it in terms of **a problem to be solved or a question to be answered.**

Problem/Callout

I want my introduction to call out *the ideal viewer for this video*, so they know it's relevant to their situation and can make a **split-second decision** about whether or not they're going to watch more.

That's why I'll often start with a question-- something like, *"Do you ever feel like..."* to introduce the problem we're going to address.

"Stick Around" Teaser

Next, I'll throw in a quick little "suspense nugget" or teaser to make sticking around for what's going to happen next a bit more enticing.

Sometimes I'll go so far as to tease both the take-home message of the video AND ALSO the next step I'll be offering AFTER the video. So for example, I might say something like, *"Today, we're going to talk about how you can XYZ, **and after we're finished**, if you'd like to learn the very best way to XYZ then you're going to* *want to click on this link and go here to get my free download..."* or whatever it is you'd like them to do next.

Content

Then, **I'll go into the "meaty part" of the video right away**. I'll tell them what they tuned in to learn. But quickly after that, what I want to do is **make a compelling case for the NEXT step** by doing what I call *"identifying the gap."*

One way to *make sure that there IS a gap to identify* is to use the content portion of your video to point out the possibility that **the thing your viewer *thinks* the problem is, is not actually the *real* problem.**

This won't always be relevant or effective, *but when it is, it works like a charm!*

"Next Step" Teaser

This is *so important.*

You have to **make sure they know what's still missing** from the picture. You have to make sure they're aware that *your video did NOT provide a complete and permanent solution* to their underlying problem (which it probably didn't, because let's be honest-- 3 minute videos don't usually end up creating massive levels of change in people's lives).

But if you're not careful, **your viewer could still actually believe that they got everything they needed from you or everything you had to offer** by the time your video ends.

That's why *there still has to be some suspense there--* **something that feels incomplete.** If the viewer feels like they're "done", they'll have no reason to want to do the NEXT thing you're asking them to do.

So you've got to *show them the gap.* Now that your video has BEGUN to address their problem, you've got to make sure they know **what they REALLY need in order to get the solution they tuned in to get** (which, hopefully, *will be your freebie or possibly* *your product or service).*

That's how you get them to take the next step.

Call to Action

Now that your viewer knows WHY they should take the next step, as you finish your video you'll want to **make it *very clear* WHAT the viewer should do next** if they really want the benefit you've promised (*or at least hinted at*) in the previous step.

For your average sales video, this structure should suffice-- however, if you're creating something more substantial like a 90 minute webinar, there are some other elements and nuances you might want to include.

However, that's a big and meaty can of worms we won't have time to open in this particular book.

For now, I want to address a question I'm asked a lot about this stuff: *"How long should my video be?"*

My response?

As long as it needs to be to say what you need to say, and nothing more.

But then of course, you might then wonder **what, exactly, do you NEED to say** *to make a sale?*

The best way to know that is to actually go out and *have some sales conversations* so you can find out.

Make a mental note of any **questions or objections that come up**, and how you addressed them (or could have addressed them).

If they're coming up in your conversations, *chances are your video viewers are thinking them as well*, so it's best to plan for that.

Generally, the bigger your "ask", *the more you should expect the prospect to need to hear* before they're ready to buy.

In other words, you don't need a 90 minute video to sell a $27 masterclass-- but you might need that long to sell a membership in a hundred thousand dollar mastermind.

Make sense?

Good! Moving on, then.

● ●

How much help/information/STUFF should I give away for free?

While providing value for free is a very important component of building trust throughout your sales funnel, the only way to get great results is to have a clear understanding of exactly *what sorts of value* **to provide (and NOT provide)** for maximum persuasive power.

If you're putting a ton of time and effort into creating, sharing and promoting your content, you might have wondered...

"Am I giving away too much?"

"How do I know when to give it away and when to make them pay?"

Here's the deal, guys.

Suspense works. Curiosity works.

Making it clear that a piece of the puzzle (possibly the MOST important piece) is missing could mean the difference between making a sale and... well, *not.*

However, *we can't hold back the best of what we have to offer* and assume that people are going to trust that we know what we're talking about.

After all, the point of sharing all of this content in the first

place is to prove that you DO know what you're talking about.

And you know what else?

That "most important piece" that's going to be missing from the free content you share?

It's almost always going to fall into one of the following three categories: *support, context and implementation.*

So I can share with you some of the best of what I know about marketing, for example, but **if I'm not personally coaching you through it**, you won't have the support or clarity you might need to *apply what you've learned effectively* (let alone *troubleshoot it* if the results aren't showing up the way you expected).

Over the course of the next year, I might share 100 free videos and give you *a virtual encyclopedia of marketing knowledge*, **but without the proper context** (an understanding of what to focus on or change and when, *based on your unique situation*), you might get totally overwhelmed and *not do anything*, **or** *do things in the wrong order* and not get the results you want.

I can tell you from my own experience that after consuming just about **every piece of free information I could get my hands on**, *it wasn't until I finally bit the bullet and got help* from people who were getting the kinds of results I wanted that things started to actually work.

Can you piece together some good results on free information alone?

Probably. Some people can.

I was not one of them.

Don't get me wrong, I learned a TON-- but **it's not the knowing that matters**, in the end. *It's the way you put together the things you know* that really counts.

I had a friend tell me once that anyone can follow instructions from a cookbook, but *a master chef can consistently create something delicious--* **with or without a recipe.**

My take on this? Feel free to share as much helpful information as you'd like-- so long as you always make it clear that **there's magic happening behind the curtain**, AND give them a compelling reason to *check it out sooner rather than later.*

Truth is, the specific position of the "free line" (*where you draw the line between free and paid assistance*) **depends entirely on what you sell.** This is one of those subtle nuances that really could make or break your sales process, and it's not something that can be easily spelled out in a book.

If you're not exactly sure which pieces of "magic" to hold behind the curtain or the "free line", not to worry-- simply visit the link at the end of this book and I'll be happy to help out. Ok? Ok.

Now, let's talk about one of my FAVORITE subjects in the whole wide world...

Chapter Eight:
How to Effortlessly Drive Traffic to Your Content So You NEVER Have to Cold Call/Social Media Stalk Anyone, Ever Again

Show Me!

How to Get (the Right Sorts of) Eyeballs on Your Content-- Whether You Pay for Ads or Not

First of all, let it be known that **I LOVE pay-per-click advertising**, and at the time of this writing, *I am loving (and getting massively awesome results from) Facebook ads in particular.*

The reason I love them is that I love the idea that I get to choose **who's watching my videos, when they watch them** *and* **what they do next.**

Knowing that most new people in my audience are coming from my Facebook ads, I am currently focusing most of my organic marketing efforts on Facebook as well.

Since most of my clients ALSO have audiences that frequently use Facebook, I typically recommend that they post a new secondary selling video on Facebook at least once a week. *Of course, more is always better if you can swing it.*

The great thing about sharing videos on Facebook is that it gives you the opportunity to *build a warm audience*, **or an audience of people who are already familiar with what you do (which, as we've already discussed, is** *one of the most important marketing assets you could have.***)**

I'm sure you've heard marketers saying that "the money is in the list", and when they say that, they typically mean the email list. **What I'd like to propose is something a bit more radical.** Truth is, *it's getting harder and harder to sell via email.* I think that as marketers, *we need to start getting a little more creative* simply because everybody's inboxes are so full.

That's why I believe that it's *so important* to build up a warm audience of **people you can pay to get your content out in front of.**

When you share videos from your business page, Facebook

gives you the opportunity down the road to *show ads specifically to the people who've watched your videos.*

So where before, the best thing you could do was target, maybe, *the small handful of people who've visited your website,* **now you can build up a warm audience *so much faster and so much more inexpensively* because your videos are going to be seen by so many more people.**

I would recommend considering this now, even if you feel like you're not even CLOSE to being ready to run paid ads yet. *Facebook will save data about your business page's video viewers either way,* so you don't have to figure it all out right this minute in order to benefit from it some time in the future.

• •

Facebook Groups and DOLLA BILLS

Another great way to get your videos seen (not to mention build a community and a culture around your brand) is to **start a Facebook group that's centered on a certain topic.**

Making the name of your group about that topic can be helpful because *that way new members will know exactly what to expect* in terms of what content you'll be sharing with them.

And here's why **most Facebook groups are LAME**, and why yours is going to be so much better.

Most Facebook groups do the same thing, and the people in those groups are getting a little bored of it.

Everybody does those stale, boring, "Day of the Week" posts that everybody knows are pre-scheduled and not posted in there by a human.

I would love to see more marketers treating their Facebook Groups more like the intimate, supportive communities of

like-minded individuals they were originally designed to be.

I would love to see marketers *engaging in their groups in a more real, authentic way* and *posting things that are different, interesting, funny, exciting or inspiring*. If you do that, you can **set your group apart** as a place where the content really is valuable.

The reason I love to share my videos in my Facebook group as opposed to on my page alone is because **my group members are typically much more likely to see them** than just the people who at one point clicked "like" on my business page. As I mentioned before, the organic reach of content posted on business pages is just *nowhere near where it used to be*, so this is **one of many great ways to adapt** to that shift.

Of course, outside of Facebook ads, pages and groups, it can also be helpful to post your content on other platforms as well...

• •

My Lesser-Known Love on Social Media: *Pinterest*

I love Pinterest as a marketing platform because a) I know my audience is there, but also because b) by the very nature of the way the platform is set up, **good content on Pinterest gets shared substantially more (*and for longer*) than it does on most other social networks**. Where on other platforms, once you scroll past something you're unlikely to see it again, I still see content I first saw YEARS ago getting "pinned" and "repinned" thousands of times over even today.

Even though Pinterest's algorithm continues to change and will most likely make it harder and harder for new pinners to gain traction (as is most often the case with content saturation), **the viral sharing that goes on there is still most definitely worth taking advantage of** if you suspect you might have an active contingent of Pinterest users in your audience.

One cool thing about running paid ads on Pinterest is that **if people pin your ad** (which they will if it's any good...) **then you don't have to pay for it to be shown to their followers!** If your ad goes viral on Pinterest (which it totally might, simply because of the way the platform works) then you could end up selling lots of stuff to people you NEVER HAD TO PAY A DIME to get in front of!

Super cool, yes?

Another thing you might want to consider about Pinterest (as well as other more visually-focused social networks like Instagram) is that depending on what you sell, **you might be able to get away with a lot *less* personality marketing** and relationship building than you might think before you can start making the sort of money you're after...

• •

Selling Stuff and Visual Platforms: Personality Optional?

If what you sell is something that fits into the *"I see it, therefore I want it"* category, paying for more direct "straight to the sale" ads *could possibly be* the right course of action for you.

POSSIBLY.

Your big challenge then becomes *building a relationship during your customer experience--* **making the process so positive and so memorable** that you create a customer for life.

In large part, this will depend on what you do to follow up with past customers, which is why so many business owners rely heavily on automation-- this enables them to reliably and systematically make sure they're continually offering opportunities to return and buy more.

I'm STILL going to recommend a "personality first" approach

more often than not, though, because really I do think **it's a more effective way to stay competitive long-term** in a crowded market, no matter WHAT you sell.

But you probably already know that by now... right?

• •

10 Rookie Mistakes I Made w/PPC Ads

My pay-per-click ad results used to suck BUTT, guys.

Big, fat, hairy BUTT.

One time I spent $120 to get one measly little lead for my marketing services company-- and **he didn't even buy anything!**

You guys, I have had *so many failed ad campaigns*, it's not even funny.

Getting a positive return on the money you invest in ads is a hard thing to do.

But **it can be done**. It is being done, incredibly successfully, by people just like you, all over the world, all the time.

Now, I'm creating a positive return on my ad spend **without breaking a sweat,** *and helping my clients do the same.*

And before I can even begin to explain to you what eventually worked for me, I figure I should probably first tell you **what *didn't* work.**

After all, there's no reason why you should have to repeat the same mistakes I made, right? *Nobody should have to suffer that kind of agony.*

It's just *inhumane.*

After running *hundreds of campaigns* and **spending thousands and thousands of dollars** on Facebook, Instagram, Pinterest, Twitter, YouTube, Google Search, Google Display, LinkedIn and even Reddit, I wanted to share with you some of the things I had to learn the hard way so you can save yourself some of the heartache I had to go through during the "trial and error" phase of things.

The following are 10 of the biggest mistakes I made-- hopefully now *you won't have to repeat them!*

10. I Did What I Was "Supposed To" Do

As a rookie advertiser, I thought the safest bet would be to just **copy the structure of the ads I saw in my news feed.**

Simple enough, right?

There's only one problem-- when all the ads look the same, people start to ignore them. *They're no longer interesting.*

Not to mention, while I might have had the structure right, there were a TON of subtleties within the ad process that at the time I had no clue about that undoubtedly killed my ad performance.

One such subtlety was this...

9. I Bid With My Heart Instead of My Head

Once upon a time, my bidding strategy was very sophisticated. It went a little something like this. I would get *what I thought was a **brilliant idea*** for an ad.

I would think to myself *"This is the ONE! This is the magical ad that's going to change my life!"* and I would be in such a hurry to see that magic that I would put way too much money behind it rather than testing a bunch of different smaller variations and gradually scaling up the best performers.

So then when I didn't double my money the first day, **I would panic and shut it down.**

Nowadays, I know better. **Slow and steady**. *Testing. Patience.* It's not sexy, but it's better. *Trust me.*

8. I Went Wide Instead of Deep

You've heard it before-- **try to please everybody and you'll end up pleasing *nobody*.**

But here's one you might not have heard: *multi-platform advertising is **not** for rookies.*

When I was just starting out, I thought it was all about finding the platform where the results would be the best, so I developed tons of campaigns *on every online ad platform under the sun.*

And of course, I knew enough to get the importance of targeting, but at that point I was still missing a much more important piece of the puzzle-- **REtargeting**.

"All You Need to Know to Get Started with Ad Targeting"

thebookonpersonalitymarketing.com/video-6

It's so much more effective to **build a deeper relationship with a smaller, more specific audience over time** than it is to *spray your message across a dozen different channels to a bunch of different audiences* to see where it'll stick.

That's why now, I almost always recommend that my clients begin by using either Facebook or Google ads (*and, on occasion, Promoted Pins*) because the retargeting options there are so much more advanced, and then of course **once things are working like you want them to**, then you can start experimenting on other platforms.

7. I Blamed the Algorithm

When your ads aren't working, you might feel tempted to blame the algorithm of whatever ad platform you're using. Every day I hear marketers whining, *"Something's wrong with Facebook, my costs are getting higher"* or *"Facebook hates me! They're not showing my ads!"*

Here's the problem with thinking about it like that.

It leaves you powerless.

These days, *I take full responsibility* for my ad performance-- **and so should you.**

Even if you're working with an agency, because **no one can obsess about your business like you do.**

And you know what? Sometimes, while I'm investigating things (*because I assume I must have made a mistake somewhere that needs correcting*) I'll **find that a link isn't working**, or notice that **my headline makes no sense on mobile** because I forgot to check the proper device preview before I launched the campaign.

That's stuff I never would have checked if I had just said something like *"Well, clearly Facebook hates me so I might as well quit this business and move back to Hoboken."*

I'm not actually *from* Hoboken... but I'm sure it's very nice there.

They have a fire museum.

So... that's cool.

6. I Didn't Know My Platforms Well Enough

One big thing I learned from all my ad shenanigans?
Every social network has its own personality and its own set of
best practices.

I had no business running Reddit ads when I first tried that,
for example. **I don't *use* Reddit**. You can't just read a few blog
posts and assume you understand the unique culture of a social
network you've never been a part of.

If you want to sell stuff on a social network, **spend some TIME on
that social network.** Learn what works there and what doesn't.

Otherwise, you'll probably just end up wasting your time and
money on it, like I did.

The more you can make your ads look like *some of the best
content they've seen on that particular platform*, **the better your
ad stands to perform**-- but if you don't actually know what kind
of content people really like on the ad platforms you use, how
could you possibly expect to come close?

Know your platforms, people. That's important.

5. I Put Too Much Trust In My Gut

I love guts.

Mine in particular.

I usually find them quite trustworthy... *except* when it comes to
advertising and conversion optimization.

Those things have a way of surprising you.

I can't tell you how many times *I was sure* I had come up with a better version of an ad or a landing page, only to find that the ad I thought was worse **actually performed better** than the ad I thought for sure would be the winner.

That's why now *I pay much closer attention to my conversion data, so IT can pick the winner.*

Of course, if my gut tells me to try something new, I'm still going to do it (after all, *my "ad gut" is getting smarter all the time*) but in the end, **the data always wins**-- even if my innards disagree.

4. I Tried to Be Clever

One surefire giveaway of a rookie advertiser is **cleverness** at the expense of **clarity.**

It doesn't need to sound catchy or cute.

It needs to make sense. The end.

Just kidding!

We still have 3 more!

Muahahaaaaa...

3. My Ad Scent Was Way Off

One big mistake I made early on as an advertiser was that I looked at my ads and the pages I drove traffic to *with* those ads as separate entities.

That was not smart.

Now, I see that every page in my sales funnel *needs to feel cohesive and seamless and consistent* every step of the way.

The term "ad scent" refers to the **degree to which your ad matches your landing page** (as well as *any subsequent pages* in your funnel).

This is an important thing to get right, because even the teeny tiny suspicion that *we've ended up somewhere we didn't mean to go when we clicked* can negatively impact your conversion rate.

Try it and see for yourself!

For example-- if the headline on your ad and the headline on your landing page don't match, change things up so they DO match and see what happens.
I think you'll be pleased with the results..

2. I Needed a Win Too Much

This is a big one-- lots of new advertisers have such a scarcity mentality around their marketing that *their goal is to spend as little as possible.*

That was me. **I get it.**

But now? My goal is pretty much *the opposite.*

I actually want to **spend** as much as possible, because 1) *I know my funnels are consistently producing a nice healthy return on what I invest*, and 2) *because I know that ad costs are only going to increase* as more and more people start jumping on board, so **even if I just broke even** on what I spent, **it would still feel like a win** because *a highly engaged audience is an incredibly valuable asset* not just in the short term, but the long term as well.

When you play "not to lose" instead of playing to win with ads, you don't give your ads or your audience the chance to mature and optimize and refine themselves over time.

You push for the **quick result** and skimp on other investments that could have, in the long run, produced better results for you *if you had been patient enough* to let it all play out.

Don't DO it, man! Don't be afraid to lose some money at first while you're figuring things out. That's a normal part of the process and it's totally OK.

Just watch, learn, and get better as you go.

And if you get *really scared or frustrated,* **come talk to me.** I can help. ;)

1. I Didn't Use Video

You had to know that video would be my #1, right?

Video has, by leaps and bounds, been *the best and most profitable addition to my marketing strategy* to date, and here's why I think that is.

Because as we've established, social media today is SO RIDICULOUSLY saturated with content!

As a result, it becomes harder all the time to get people's attention-- and *even harder still* to get them to buy.

The reason video is so powerful is that *it gives the viewer the chance to see what you're really like* so they can decide if they like and trust you enough to buy from you.

With video, the feeling of rapport *that would have taken years to develop using blog posts alone* can instead take place **over a period of days or even MINUTES**, which means you can turn strangers into customers *much faster than you otherwise could have.*

It's pretty danged cool.

That's not to mention the fact that at least right now, **if you know what you're doing**, running video ads will most likely be quite *a bit less expensive for you* than image-based ads.

• •

"But I don't WANNA figure out how to run PPC ads!"

If that's what you're thinking right now, let's talk about that for a second, ok?

You CAN be successful without them. **You really can.**

But tactical stuff aside, what I'm more concerned about when I hear this sort of objection from people is *their mindset.*

"Playing it safe" is a death sentence, as far as I'm concerned, for today's marketer.

> **There is NOTHING SAFE about small thinking.**
>
> **There is NOTHING SAFE about hiding from the reality of the world we live in.**
>
> **There is NOTHING SAFE about refusing to learn what you need to know to succeed in a big way.**
>
> **There is NOTHING SAFE about shooting for a *little bit of success.***
>
> **There is NOTHING SAFE about quitting as soon as things get scary.**

Let's just make that very clear right now.

If your business really is just a hobby, that's different. I guess.

But I'll tell you the truth... *if it **is** just a hobby, I don't get it.*

Why just *play at* business when you could CHANGE THE WORLD?

Why just *test the waters* when you could *dive in, head first?*

I know it feels risky. It IS risky.

But you know what's even riskier?

Being a WUSS.

Why couldn't you play to WIN? Why couldn't you decide to change the game in your industry as soon as NOW?

You CAN! And if we only get ONE SHOT at life as we know it... **are you going to live (and market) like an A-Lister, or are you going to live (and market) like a POTATO PERSON?**

Ok. Pardon the outburst... *I get excited about this stuff.*

I just wish you could see what I see when I look at you... when I talk to you guys on social media and see how much passion you have for the things you love and the people you serve. It's INCREDIBLY inspiring and I'm HONORED to know you!

But I sometimes wonder...

What would happen if you were to PUMP UP THAT PASSION and turn it into a FULL-BLOWN OBSESSION?

What would change about the way you think about your business? Your goals? Your time? Your future?

Would you be a chicken about running ads then, too?

What I love about pay-per-click ads is the SPEED at which you can learn what to do and what not to do.

I love that (if you know how to make sense of your data,) ads give you the information you need to *quickly adapt your plan as you go,* so that you don't have to spend years building a product and a following and networking and blogging **only to figure out that you were in entirely the wrong business** in the first place.

You can get that information (and take action on it) *SO much sooner.*

And while patience is very important with this sort of thing, **speed and momentum** can be very important as well.

Anyway, back to the practical stuff ... if you're using video in your ads, *I strongly recommend also using captions*. That way your message will make sense, even if people don't want to watch with the sound (which is usually the case).

Then, it's just a matter of **making sure that ad gets out in front of the right people**, as well as playing with Facebook's algorithm a bit to get the best possible cost per lead. You'll need to experiment with things to see where your message is going to perform the best.

But, so I can make sure your head doesn't explode at this point, I'll go ahead and stop there.

• •

How to Scale Your Organic Traffic Strategy and "Be Everywhere" (Without Going Insane)

Paid ads aside, with the ever-increasing array of marketing platforms popping up online today, things can get pretty overwhelming pretty quickly-- especially when you've got marketers telling you that the key to your *"world domination strategy"* is to **be everywhere.**

- Instagram
- Snapchat
- Facebook
- Twitter
- Pinterest
- LinkedIn
- Blogging
- Podcasting
- Email marketing
- Messenger
- SMS
- ALL THE PLACES, ALL THE THINGS!

It's no wonder your average business owner is *exhausted, overwhelmed and confused.*

When I work with clients, I advise them to look at their marketing *kind of like a financial planner looks at your investment portfolio--* in the beginning, you should start out by investing in just one or two things, and then **as you grow, you can diversify.**

If you're a creative type like I am and your brain starts to fry *at the mere thought of math-related stuff*, let me tell you what I mean by diversifying your marketing investments.

I see way too many business owners *spreading themselves painfully thin*, trying to market their stuff on **every social media platform**, trying to push out *a bunch of different offers* at the same time, which means their energy, focus and resources are too scattered to get meaningful results with any one thing.

That's why I'm a big fan of trying *one new offer*, *one new funnel* and/or *one new platform at a time*, making sure it's a good use of resources, then gradually **expanding out** from there.

That way *we'll focus your precious time and resources* on the stuff that's going to make the **biggest difference** first. That's what my "Minimum Viable Marketing" method is all about.

Earlier, I went on a tiny tirade about how **outsourcing your marketing is often a bad idea** *(which, I get, is an odd thing for someone who runs a marketing agency to say).*

What I meant was simply that **delegating the foundational work of differentiating your brand** is NOT a job for an agency or consultant. Agencies and consultants can help with that stuff, most definitely, but if you're expecting them to wave a magic wand and make you rich... *that's not what we're here to do.*

Marketing consultants and agencies are not miracle workers, but we DO (or at least SHOULD) know how to take your *good* ideas and make them *great,* and take *brands and products that are already cool* and position them as *extraordinary.*

Once you've done the all-important work of figuring out how to set yourself apart and create engaging content *(with or without the help of someone like me)* what you most certainly CAN and SHOULD outsource is the DISTRIBUTION of that content.

We call this your *organic* traffic strategy, in that we're sharing your content as a means of bringing new leads into your funnel, but **not necessarily paying money** to get that in front of a specific audience.

The best way I know to leverage your time and resources efficiently and "be everywhere" *without going totally nuts* is to employ what I call **the "cornerstone content" strategy.**

• •

How to Save TONS of Time with Cornerstone Content

This is how MY PERSONAL content creation strategy works.

At the beginning of the week, I make 1-3 videos.

I send them off to my team.

My team **edits** them, puts **captions** on them, designs **graphics** for them, turns them into **blog posts**, **podcast episodes** and a variety of **other juicy snippets** to share on my chosen handful of the major social networks.

They can do that **without compromising our marketing message** because the content *originated* with me-- my storytelling, my enthusiasm, my nerdiness-- which means that no matter what they might do to slice and dice and repurpose it, it's still going to have a consistent, cohesive brand identity.

That's a GREAT way to outsource **without delegating away *too* much.**

You can outsource your ad management, your funnel execution, your conversion optimization, your media outreach, any *number* of marketing-related tasks, *so long as you know what success looks like* **and you don't expect results to be "given" to you by the person or people you hire.**

I say this because ALL THE TIME I have business owners coming to me for help because (they tell me) some other marketer made all sorts of lofty promises *but didn't deliver results.*

When I ask them further questions, it becomes clear that in *almost every case* where this happened, the business owner forked over a large sum of money **before they ever established a powerful strategy for differentiating their brand/product**, answered a few quick onboarding questions and then sat back expecting a miracle.

Of COURSE the results didn't show up!

Really nailing your marketing strategy is no small feat, my friend. I would advise you to **take a very active role** in that process, or it's highly likely that you'll be disappointed.

If you don't have the slightest clue what you're doing, marketing-wise?

You're a business owner. Selling stuff is your JOB. **Learn how to do it.** *THEN get help. Your results will be SOOOO much better for it, trust me.*

Our most successful clients are ALWAYS those who come to us because they're **already having some success** and they're ready to have more.

If you're barely getting started, chances are, *what you need is coaching or consulting first.* Figure out (and more importantly, *test*) your content and funnel strategy, then you can hire all the help in the world **to ignite, troubleshoot and ideally SKYROCKET what's already starting to work for you.**

Chapter Nine:
What To Do If You Try Everything I Tell You and It STILL Doesn't Seem To Be Working

Help Me!

"I think my videos are good... why aren't people paying attention?"

Want to get more attention from your videos?

Outside of paying for that attention, your ONLY OPTION is to become so captivating in your videos that the people who watch them *just KNOW* that they need more of YOU in their lives.

And where most people go wrong here is they think all it takes to be captivating is the surface-level stuff, like the script, the lighting, the editing and the camera wizardry they use.

Listen up, guys:

Even if you do everything "by the book," *you could still lose out on sales* because your video viewers just "don't feel right" about you.

They don't know why, but **they don't trust you.**

Or maybe they DO trust you, but they *feel like they can't relate to you* or *you don't make them feel comfortable.*

All of these things matter just as much if not WAY MORE than the content in your videos or the angles you use or the lighting or the editing or any of that stuff.

It's what's beneath the surface that really tells the story.

Because, think about it-- if you're saying all the right stuff **but you look totally uncomfortable**, nobody's going to notice what you're saying. *They're going to feel uncomfortable.*

Or if you're too low-energy or too high-energy or whatever energy you've got doesn't match up with the way your viewer needs to feel, *you're going to lose them.*

It's these subtle nuances that make all the difference in the success or failure of your videos. For example...

Have you ever seen a commercial that was ALMOST funny? Like they were trying really hard to be funny, but they didn't quite get there?

It's like watching a car wreck, isn't it?

Or maybe you watched a video one time that was trying to tug at your heartstrings with some dramatic testimonials or somebody's sob story, but *it didn't really feel genuine, so you felt totally manipulated?*

Subtle things like that can make a HUGE difference in the way viewers respond to your videos, **especially when it comes time to make a purchase decision**, and the fanciest editing software in the world can't make people trust you.

Bottom line: *if you want your videos to make an impact on your viewer, you've got to do whatever it takes to* **show up on camera and BE the kind of person who makes an impact!**

And you know what?

It's not NEARLY as hard as it sounds!

Being the right kind of person is as simple as forgetting whatever mental garbage your inner potato-person is spewing out at you and **staying in a spirit of genuine love, service and empathy for your viewer.**

Bad on-camera performances pretty much all stem from the same cause, and that's *fear, selfishness and insecurity.* Those are things that absolutely can be eliminated, even if only for a few minutes, by forgetting about YOU and bringing it back to THEM.

It might sound scary or confusing, but the good news is, **if you keep at it for long enough to get the hang of it, it'll become second nature to you.** You can do it *every time* and it's going to feel totally effortless.

I promise.

• •

"I'm Doing EVERYTHING RIGHT... Why Isn't It Working?"

Of course, without knowing specifics it's really hard for me to answer a question like that, but I CAN tell you that 99% of the time if you're trying to make money with online marketing and it's not working, it's for one of these two reasons: *#1: because your offer isn't different enough, in the right ways* and/or *#2: because YOU are not different enough, in the right ways.*

Being different in the right way-- that's it. That's the whole game.

If you can master that, you win.

So, to make things a little bit clearer for you, let's break this idea down into some smaller pieces, shall we? Four pieces, to be exact.

1: Your offer isn't different enough.

The things that tend to really sell well *no matter WHAT you do marketing-wise* are the products and services that nobody else is offering yet. If you can be *one of the first to market with something really awesome*, your job, marketing wise, is SO much easier than the rest of ours.

Congratulations!

BUT you can still run into trouble if...

2: Your offer isn't different enough IN THE RIGHT WAYS.

Being first-to-market with a product like *artificial toe fungus*... that might not be all that lucrative.

That said, there may or may not be a market for artificial toe fungus!

I don't know, maybe for novelty stores or something?

Sometimes **you don't know if your offer is different in the right way** until you put it in front of people and let the market tell YOU.

Years before I started NerdyGirl.co, I started a company selling faux-fur floor beds to parents like me, who were more on the "crunchy" side and didn't want to do the crib thing for their kiddos.

I couldn't get them to sell.

Maybe that was just because I didn't know as much about marketing then as I do now, but alas, for whatever reason, **I couldn't make it work.**

Who knew?

I couldn't have really known until I put it out there and gave it a try.

So I tried it. It didn't work. I moved on.

That's entrepreneurship.

Welcome to the jungle, home slice.

3. YOU aren't different enough

Of course, "you" might really mean YOU and your personal brand, or it could mean a company or product brand. For our purposes here, I'll just say YOU.

This is where most of us need to play *because most of us don't have something all that new and different to offer,* and that's okay-- **if you can be smart about it.**

Just in a single day on Facebook, I swear, I saw no less than 5 different ads for how to get X amount of coaching clients or make X amount of money in X amount of time.

BARF.

Where's the personality, guys?

Where's the proof?

Why should I pick YOU out of the five random coaches who coach coaches about coaching?

NOW HEAR THIS, MARKETERS: **GONE are the days when you can just throw up a "me too" ad and a "me too" funnel and turn a profit.** There are just TOO MANY PEOPLE competing for the same customers.

> **Your ads have got to be extraordinary.**
>
> **Your *brand* has got to be extraordinary.**
>
> **Your *content* has *got* to be EXTRAORDINARY!**

And it's not about new ideas. *There ARE no new ideas.* It's not even really about new products or services, because these days there aren't that many of those either!

If you sell the same old stuff everybody else sells, that's okay, *just know that your "likeability factor" and your "after-ness" and the specificity of the offers and the content you're putting in front of people* have NEVER been more important.

Which brings me to the final (and possibly the most important) piece...

4: Your brand isn't different enough IN THE RIGHT WAYS

It's simple.

The reason so many people are taking so many courses on marketing and branding and advertising and sales and STILL not getting results is that *they're either not implementing what they're learning*, OR they ARE implementing, but *they're thinking that somebody else's "proven system" is going to do all the work* for them, rather than **taking the burden of originality upon themselves.**

And while these proven systems and strategies and tactics can be great and helpful and effective, *they can only get you so far*.

At a certain point, **it's up to YOU to set yourself apart**, and to figure out HOW to set yourself apart *in a way that actually will make people want to buy what you sell*.

So, how do you do that? Here are just a few of the MANY possible ways you might be able to set your brand, your offer, your message and your content apart from your competitors.

Are you ready? Let's count them down from ten.

10. You can be hotter sauce than your competitors

As harsh as it might sound to us "average-looking humans", *this can make a difference*.

We can't all change our looks, but if you're great looking, USE it!

People love good looking people, successful people and, dare I say, rich people.

If you've got it, flaunt it. **That's showbiz.**

9. You can say what nobody else is saying.

Method did this when they changed the conversation about cleaning products.

Before, it was all about "is it effective"?

Now, it's about "what does it look like on my kitchen counter"?

And "does my hand soap make me look trendy and cool?"

8. You can have the best visuals

Can't be the best looking?

No biggie...

Go for the best graphics or the best video quality or the most stylish setting for your videos.

Visuals matter big-time, so *do whatever you can to make yours appealing* and eye-catching (without, of course, being obnoxious).

7. You can be more generous

This is how Toms exploded onto the scene.

People love feeling like the things they buy are *making the world a better place*, so you might want to consider how to add some sort of charitable element to your brand promise.

Just be aware that you need to demonstrate you **actually CARE about what you say you care about**, or you'll risk *looking like a self-serving poser.*

6. You can be funnier

Of course, comedy is a great way to make your content more engaging.

However, *it can also undermine your credibility*, if you're not careful, so **make sure to use comedy wisely**.
Remember-- "almost funny" *could be worse* than not funny at all.

5. You can be more likeable

Whether or not you incorporate comedy into your marketing, **being more approachable than your competitors** can make a huge difference. There are a few ways you can do that-- you can *embrace and even call attention to your imperfections* (blooper reels are my favorite way to do that), you can *present a more honest, balanced point of view* than your audience is used to seeing, or you can just *take a subject that most people find complicated and simplify it*; make it easier to understand.

The key here is to *be yourself* and **enjoy what you're doing**.

The more fun you're having, the more we'll enjoy your content.

4. You can tell a better story

Stories sell, guys-- but *what sorts of stories?*

The best stories for selling are the stories that enable us to *draw parallels between the lives of the characters and our own lives--* **they give us a vision of what's possible**.

When we can really envision the ups and downs, the challenges this character has overcome, **the cool stuff they've been able to experience on the other side**-- that's when we really start to want to jump in and *make the story into OUR story.*

If you can get really good at telling stories like those-- whether they come from your life, your clients' lives, your customers' lives or even the life of an imaginary character-- you'll be able to sell your stuff *a whole lot more easily.*

3. You can speak to a more specific audience

If the thing you offer has a really broad potential audience, you might want to consider creating multiple pieces of "bait" to promote as you grow, each directed at *a different subset of that larger audience.*

The more specific you get about *who your content is for*, the more compelled that audience will be to watch it because **we're psychologically predisposed to look for whatever seems to be the most relevant thing in our line of sight.**

If I'm a chiropractor, for example, I would be a lot more likely to watch a video about *accounting for chiropractors* than I would be to watch a video about accounting for *business owners in general.*

2. You can address a more specific problem

Another way to take advantage of the power of specificity is to *get more specific about the problem you're solving.* Let me give you an example.

One of my students teaches practical coping skills to parents of special needs families. A while back, she shared a video with the title **"3 Tips for Dinner Time."**

My feedback to her was that 1) that headline doesn't tell me anything about what sort of tips I'll be getting, and 2) it also doesn't tell me whether or not those tips will be relevant to my unique situation.

She changed it to: **"Sensory Processing Disorder at the Dinner Table: 3 Simple Ways to Keep the Peace."**

See? *Soooo much clearer!*

Headlines are huge, because in most cases that's the only chance you're going to get to give scrollers by a reason to choose you instead of all the other exciting things demanding their attention-- so *it's on you* to make a compelling case for why YOU deserve a piece of their precious time.

Oh, and by the way, *when you GET "a piece of that precious time"?*

You *cannot* squander it.

You *cannot* ramble, you *cannot* be self-indulgent and you *must* add value-- or you'd better believe the next time that same person scrolls by your stuff, **they won't be stopping again.**

So *get your game face on, guys.*

The best content wins, so **make yours the best.**
Which brings me to my final (and favorite) way to set your content apart from everybody else's...

1. You can address a problem in a more engaging way

Fact: if your content is not engaging, not only will your viewers NOT come back for more, **they will also be *highly unlikely* to buy from you.**

This is *especially* true for video content.

Now, why won't they buy from you if they're not engaged and entertained by your video content?

Because they're never going to *finish it!*

They're going to get bored, drop off and leave *before you ever get to the part* where you talk about the thing you have to sell.

Or, even if for some reason *they're just that bored* or you're just that concise or for whatever reason they DO stick around and finish watching your video, *they won't have a strong enough emotional connection to your message* to take action.

If you feel like you've "tried everything", **let me guess what you've *really tried.***

> You've watched like 36 webinars.

> You've taken a course. Maybe two.

Maybe you even hired a coach.

You've implemented some of the stuff you've learned, but not all of it.

Not the stuff that seems REALLY hard or scary.

Maybe you've spent about a hundred bucks on ads, but you shut them down when you didn't make 300 bucks back within the first three days.

And that's great.

That's a great start, and it's farther than a lot of people get... but if you're not getting the results, you have not tried hard enough, long enough, or well enough.

There *is no failure* here. I no longer acknowledge the existence of failure because I believe in the importance of patience.

So I don't want you to beat yourself up.

Maybe this process takes you two tries, *maybe it takes you two hundred.*

Every time you try, you'll get better.

If you feel like you need another course or a coach to help fill in the gaps in what you know, **that's fine.** Go learn what you need to learn, get the mentorship you need to feel confident. *Or don't.*

But either way, there's only one way to shortcut this process.

SHOW UP.

> *Show up and make people feel stuff.*

> *Show up and help people.*

> *Show up and entertain people.*

Show up and be so good they cannot ignore you and they cannot forget you.

Show up and make offers.

If people don't buy them, make different offers or make the same offer in a different way. *Make mistakes. Learn.* **Adjust.**

The only way this super-complicated "show up" system will NOT ultimately work for you is *if you show up and annoy everyone* with the same tired, boring, meaningless, sales-y content. **But even then, it might still work.**

Because showing up is *that* powerful.

• •

Help! I'm Getting Attention, but... Why Is Nobody Buying!?

If your content seems to be performing pretty well as far as engagement goes, but you're not seeing any change in your bank account, that can be a tricky problem to address.

Never fear, *NerdyGirl is here* to help!

Selling and entertaining is a subtle and sometimes complex thing, and *it's not at all easy* to master. However, there are some *predictable patterns you can count on* as you put together your ads, videos, sales pages and any other marketing or sales-related assets you plan to put in place to grow your business.

Inevitably you're going to need to answer the following three questions in your prospect's mind before you can successfully make a sale: *why this, why you, and why now*?

Why This?

If we want to get people to pay attention to our content, we first have to know **how to make our content seem relevant, interesting and attractive** *to the right kind of viewer.*

This is the primary job that your headline needs to do, so that the reader or viewer can discern as quickly as possible *what's in it for them.*

"Why this" is the question that depends the most on *your belief in (and your ability to explain) what's so great about your product or service* because the more certain YOU feel about it, the more likely we'll be to believe you.

From the very first second your prospect reads your headline or sees your face, *they're going to pick up on the emotional energy* you're putting behind it.

It might sound weird, but *trust me, it matters.*

By the way, having a great deal of confidence in the value of what you have to offer can also impact *the amount you'll be able to charge for it*, if you're in a position to make pricing decisions.

This is about more than just mindset, too-- it's about your ability to **eloquently and powerfully explain the benefits** of what you offer to your prospect so there's no mistaking the fact that it's worth every penny.

A big part of that, of course, is knowing what makes your particular offer *different from others like it.*

Which brings me to your prospect's second question...

Why You?

Once you've made a compelling case for your product or service, another major thing you'll need to consider if you want to persuade someone to buy the thing you offer is this: *why should they buy that thing from YOU* instead of someone else?

This is the question that depends the most on *your belief in yourself* as well as the strength and clarity of your personal brand.

And again, allow me to remind you that this *DOES NOT AT ALL depend* on you having a particular degree, a particular certification, or even having some sort of "picture perfect life" that everybody wants.

This is simply about figuring out what you DO have to offer that's special and making sure your marketing makes that clear.

One of the most important things to consider when it comes to setting yourself apart is that it's a lot less about you than you might think.

The most powerful way to position yourself as **the clear and best choice in your industry**, *especially early on*, is to *make your message more specific*-- that's the easiest way I know to establish yourself as a specialist, which tends to have much higher perceived value than someone with a more diluted, general message, offer and audience.

There are tons of ways to encourage potential buyers to choose you *that are 100% within your control.*

> You could have a super-easy, fun, mobile-friendly checkout process.

> You could have the most engaging ads.

> You could have a sales page that reads like a Harry Potter novel.

> You could do the things that others in your field are unwilling or afraid to do.

Don't be afraid to think outside the box here, **so long as you always**

make choices with your customers' best interests in mind.

Why Now?

The last thing your prospect will be wondering (*whether they realize it or not*) is "do I really need to buy this thing now?"

I know it's obnoxious to see launch countdowns and cart closing warnings and ticking time-bombs (*I mean timers*) on so many sales pages, but the reason we put them there is because we know that **procrastination and distraction are our biggest competitors.**

Creating an authentic sense of urgency in your sales process can be a big challenge, especially if you sell a product which, by its very nature, will never go "out of stock.".

A lot of big names in my industry handle this by **perpetually launching, closing and re-launching their products** on a limited-time basis.

And while this is undoubtedly a super-effective way to create authentic urgency, *it also can take a huge amount of work,* all smushed into a relatively short period of time.

That's not to mention the fact that *when you use ads to fuel your launch, you'll have a limited window of time when you can run them*, so you'll need to know how to **quickly, efficiently and profitably scale up** your ad spend.

That is no easy task for anyone, *let alone a beginner!*

That's why I prefer to use an *evergreen urgency* model-- in other words, I don't have a specific launch period, but instead I scale up my ad campaigns gradually, while still creating urgency using evergreen countdown timers.

That way, the time left on the timer is set based on when the prospect arrives on a certain page. After the timer reaches 0, you can set it to redirect the person to another page, or you can show or hide certain elements on that same page.

That way, no matter when someone comes into my funnel, **they can still benefit from the same boost in motivation** as someone who came in three weeks later, and the time for claiming my offer *really will run out,* it'll just run out for that particular person based on the particular time they first showed up.

Whatever technique you use to create a sense of urgency around what you're selling, it's best to **be authentic and honest about it** because it can be damaging to your brand if people feel tricked.

Ultimately, while *I do think it's important* to give people a reason to take action sooner rather than later, it's something we should use tactfully and carefully.

• •

The #1 Reason an Offer Won't Sell

Brace yourself, nerdface.

I'm about to ONCE AGAIN stress the importance of a word you've already heard 54 times in this book so far (if my calculations are correct... I told you, numbers aren't my forte...)

The word is **DIFFERENT.**

If your product or service is not selling as much as you'd like it to online (or anywhere, for that matter)-- this is the *very first thing* I want you to consider.

Look objectively at your marketing message and ask: **does this appear to be something that's NEW AND DIFFERENT, or something that's merely BETTER THAN BEFORE?**

A "better than before" offer (also referred to as an *improvement* offer) is something you're selling that's *merely improving* whatever it is they're currently using or experiencing.

The best kind of offer (whether it's a freebie or a super-high-ticket paid product) is *exciting*, it's *surprising*, it's something they might've never heard of or seen before.

It can be helpful from time to time to imagine that your customer is one of those sloths from *Zootopia* and it takes them an hour to move their thumb and they'll probably get distracted and move on to something else before they ever make a decision-- which is why, **if you want your offer to be compelling enough to take action, it HAS to look new, different and exciting.**

"Better than before" offers can sell, don't get me wrong, but *they don't sell nearly as well* as new opportunities do-- just because **there's no urgency to stop what you're doing and go get something that only promises "better".**

You can sit there and rationalize, like we do about everything, "*Meh*, I'll do 'better' tomorrow."

And then you don't.

I've come to realize that this was exactly why my old sales funnels (*oh, so many funnels*) failed in the past, by the way.

I wasn't saying anything new. I was adding my voice to everybody else's.

And sure, my offers were a *little bit* different-- but they weren't **different enough** to be really compelling.

This is why clickbait works, guys.

Love it or hate it, we all secretly want to see the *shocking new study* that tells us we can **lose 28 pounds in two weeks by eating cake pops for breakfast!**

And I don't want you to stress out about this, because **here's the**

big secret-- for this to work, it doesn't have to BE new... **it just has to FEEL and SOUND and LOOK new**.

And that feeling has EVERYTHING to do with *the way you talk about it.*

This is **human nature**, guys.

We want to believe in "magic pills" and "overnight successes" and "secret sauces".

And some of you might think that's sleazy, but *here's my thought on it*: if you really believe your product or service is worth every penny (or more), then **it's your duty to do whatever is required** to make it look as appealing and extraordinary as you POSSIBLY can!

This is *not* about lying. You can do this without lying. *(And, I mean, you should... 'cause lying is bad.)*

This is about creativity.

It makes me think of *Newsies*-- in the morning when they'd go to pick up their newspapers to sell and the headlines were boring, they'd put a juicier spin on the content from the front page stories and make up new, more interesting headlines.

If they didn't do that, they'd be broke!

This is SURVIVAL, guys!

And **it's all about the headline.** Your headline is the key.

And headlines can take a lot of forms, too. The title of your video counts as a headline. So does the text on the image of your ad. So does the text at the top of your landing page.

But wherever it shows up, your headline is *the wrapping paper* around your message, the shiny (or not-so-shiny) packaging that gives us the information with which to decide whether or not we feel inclined to take a peek at what's inside the box.

It's your job to make it look different and new and special and awesome.

If you don't, *you cannot complain* and **you cannot be surprised** when your stuff doesn't sell.

I cannot tell you how awesome things become when you *really start to get the hang of* this idea.

"DIFFERENT" is the key that can unlock your success with any product, with any service, in any market. **You nail this piece and you WILL emerge victorious-- it's only a question of WHEN.**

So here's my challenge for you:

I hereby challenge you to go through all of your marketing materials-- your sales pages, your landing pages, your webinars, heck, even your blog posts, look at the headlines and the sub-headlines and and be honest with yourself-- *is it new enough?*

> *Does it feel surprising?*
> *Does it feel different?*
> *Maybe even a little bit **magical?***

And if it doesn't, I've only got one question for you-- **what are you going to do about it?**

Watch THIS

"5 Key Tests My Marketing Video Titles MUST Pass Before I Hit 'Publish'"

thebookonpersonalitymarketing.com/video-7

"Let's Assume My Funnel Works Like Gangbusters. *Then* What Do I Do?"

Once you've proven that you've got products and/or services you can sell profitably, all that's left to do is *scale it out*-- grow your following, become that household name, go out and sell more and **keep improving** upon what you've already built.

There are a bunch of different ways to do this, the first being to just *put more money into the channel where you're already doing your marketing.*

When you know where it makes sense to throw money... *throw that money, yo!*

Your typical stock market investor's jaw would drop to the FLOOR at the sight of the ROI numbers my peers and I see every day. *The potential for upside with this stuff is INSANE.*

Of course, outside of what you do with paid ads, scaling your traffic generation efforts can (and probably should) also mean experimenting with a wider variety of ad platforms, booking media appearances, bringing on affiliates, doing podcast interviews or any combination of a dozen different options.

This is where the celebrity stuff really starts cookin'-- because now that you've built a profitable business, *you should be generating enough money to pay for whatever growth strategies you need to invest in* to get as many people as possible to utterly fall in love with you and your brand.

Because, after all, that's what being a celebrity is all about, right?

As you go forth into the great wide world of fame and fortune, just think for a few minutes about where you'd like your "home base" to be-- **take your "primary pitch" URL information with you wherever you go** so that you can make the most of all of the lovely attention that's about to come your way so that *no opportunity is wasted.*

This way, all the different places you show up online can point people back to your funnel, which will get them on your email list, where you can continue to deepen those relationships and sell more and more to your subscribers over time. This is the best way to make the most of any of your public appearances so they don't just build your credibility, they also make you money.

In the scaling phase, the goal is to get *as many people talking about you and promoting you as possible*, because it's one thing for you to go out and be awesome, but it's quite another for people to tell their friends how awesome you are. **The latter is obviously a lot more powerful,** which is why the name of the game is to *give them a compelling reason to talk about you.*

What will yours be?

"5 Things That Might Get in the Way of Your Success with Personality Marketing"

thebookonpersonalitymarketing.com/video-8

Chapter Ten:

How To Create a Ridiculously Massive Return On the Tiny Investment You Made In this Book

(Instead of Putting it Down Only to Get the Same Old Lame-Sauce Marketing Results Most People Get)

WAHOO!

The Key to Getting MASSIVE Marketing Results

We've talked about why you need to be INTERESTING. We've talked about why you need to be AUTHENTIC. We've talked about why you need to be DIFFERENT.

But before I let you go, I want to make sure we talk about why perhaps, in the end, the key to your success is *actually* going to be how much you CARE.

It's not just because sincerity comes off as more persuasive in marketing videos, either.

It's because what you need MOST to make all of this stuff work is the sheer WILL to keep going, no matter what.

PERSEVERANCE. COMMITMENT. CONSISTENCY. PASSION. MOTIVATION. DRIVE.

All of those touchy-feely buzzwords you hear about in motivational speeches can be traced back to one thing; *why are you doing all of this, anyway?*

I mean, we've alluded to the fact that personality marketing is perfect for people who want to make an impact on the world, but *what does that even mean? Who is it you want to impact, and how? What change are you really trying to bring about? Why does it matter?*

If you don't have a powerful, compelling, emotionally-charged answer to those questions, you might run out of steam before you ever get the chance to see the *really cool stuff* beginning to happen.

Not to mention, that *really cool stuff* will probably start happening A WHOLE LOT SOONER **if you're filled with a** *burning* **sense of purpose, an OBSESSION even,** about what you're setting out to accomplish.

Come to think about it, **these questions are SO important to answer**, I'm going to give you a space to do just that right now...

Do This NOW

Write down your answers to the following questions:

Why are you doing all of this, anyway?

Who is it you want to impact, and how?

What change are you really trying to bring about?

Why does it matter?

• •

The Essential Business Assets You Need WAY MORE Than You Need Money

Want to know why I'm obsessed with helping you guys sell more stuff?

Here's something a bit random you should know about me:

Growing up, the message I received was,

> *"Brittany, you're going to be on Broadway."*

> *"You're going to be a famous writer."*

> *"You're going to be President."*

These were very nice messages to hear, of course. I have AMAZING parents...

...but somehow *I never really got the message that motherhood was the best/most important job.*

Maybe they said it... **maybe I just wasn't listening.**

But before I knew it, I was 24 and a new mom to my first little boy, and *I just couldn't imagine not being there* with him and for him.

So I stayed home.

And while I sat there, hopelessly in love with him, living on barely enough money to scrape by each month, *I was also going quietly insane.*

I felt, at times, like a prisoner in my own house-- only I had locked myself in and I had the keys in my hand... *I just refused to use them.*

Not sure how or where to channel my ambitions, **I found random stuff to obsess about.**

We were raw vegans for almost 3 years after I went down the "all foods will kill your children" rabbit hole.

> *I hosted a raw vegan cooking show.*

> *I obsessively created dozens of abstract art pieces for my unpaintable apartment walls.*

I wrote books nobody read, built courses nobody bought.

I wrote songs.

I wrote a musical.

And then, somewhat randomly, **I started a business.**

And that business became a different business, which became a different business again.

And as soon as (*finally!*) real money started coming in, **I was ON FIRE**.

I felt like myself again. I felt like a grownup. I wasn't counting the hours until my husband Clark got home-- for once, *I was losing track of time!*

And then **I almost blew it**. I got it wrong. Like I told you before, I came dangerously close to losing it all.

I felt like a colossal failure.

Until one day, little by little, I started to fail a little less. And then a little less.

And all of a sudden, wonder of wonders... a PROFIT!

And then... a BIG profit!

And then... bigger and bigger and "HOLY CRAP, is this for REAL?" kinda profit!

And for the first time since becoming a mother, I felt like...

THIS is what they meant when they said I could be whoever and whatever I wanted to be.

THIS is having it all.

You know… the whole work-family-personal life thing!

It was working!

I could do it!

A lot of people say their "why" is their kids… but my "why" is YOUR kids.

I believe that *happy parents raise happy kids* who go on to create a better world.

Now that I've added entrepreneurship to my career as a mother, **I feel fulfilled in a way I didn't even know I could be fulfilled.**

I'm a happier, better parent because of it.

I want that for you and your kids (if you have kids) too. If that's what YOU want, of course. **There are plenty of roads to fulfillment and I certainly would never claim that entrepreneurship is the ONLY one!**

But if you are "entrepreneurially inclined" like I am, this message is for you:

No matter how big your business gets, I want you to feel proud of the work you do and the things you accomplish.

I want the world to see how extraordinary you are.

*I want you, when all is said and done, to have felt like you made the impact you were capable of making-- **and then some.***

"Selling more stuff" is actually not what this is about, in the end.

It was never about the money for me.

I have no desire for fancy clothes or luxury cars. I love my little house at the edge of the park. I've never really cared about labels or diamonds or designer shoes or any of that hoo-ha.

Money, to me, is just one of *many possible sources of fuel* that can help get you where you aspire to go. It's not even the most important one, either.

Want to discover some sources of fuel that are even MORE POWERFUL than money? How about...

- *Hope!*
- *Excitement!*
- *Curiosity!*
- *Love for others/love for your work!*
- *The burning desire to make the most of the life you've been given!*

When you're truly connected to those sources of fuel, your intuition will show you how to get what you need.

If you have those things, you have EVERYTHING.

Entrepreneurship gives you the opportunity (and to tell you the truth, it'll FORCE you) to find those things on the road to success.

Either that, or you'll quit.

But don't quit. *You can DO this.*

And if I can play even a small part in that journey for you-- help you get there with less heartache, help you go farther, help you get there faster?

Well, dang.

That's worth waking up for.

• •

One Thing All the A-List Industry Leaders I Know Have in Common

A while back I had the opportunity to speak at an event with a bunch of super-successful women and men, and I noticed something that, at the time, seemed kinda funny.

We all wanted to hire each other-- and **a lot of us did just that!**

It was such a different feel from what I used to experience back in my "playing small" days, when everybody was trying to have success by getting what they needed **as cheaply as they possibly could**, or if at all possible, *for free.*

Now that I've started spending more and more time with high-achievers, I've noticed that they *have no problem* investing in themselves and in their businesses, because they've already experienced the results of similar investments **and feel confident that they'll get results.**

Where does this confidence come from?

Two things.

First, it comes from knowing that *when we spend time around powerful people,* **we become more powerful ourselves.**

Second, it also comes from knowing that investing in ourselves and our businesses in a big way *helps us feel SO much more motivated* to do the work that's required to get results from those investments.

We get that it's not the person or the program we're investing in that's responsible for our success, we know that **our success is entirely up to us**-- BUT we ALSO know that if we're only dipping our toe in any particular solution, *we won't value it all that much* and we probably won't do our part to make it work.

ALL of the top performers I know, across a wide variety of

industries, have made *major investments in getting support from other experts*, whether that's investing in their education, hiring consultants, joining paid masterminds, or adding new members to their teams (*usually all of the above*) and, what's more, **they openly credit those investments for a great deal of the success they've experienced.**

'Cause *here's the deal, guys--* you don't know what you don't know about your business and you can't see what you can't see about your business, so *no matter how smart, how talented or how successful you are, you can always benefit from getting an extra pair of eyes* on your work. You can ALWAYS benefit from hearing someone else's brilliant ideas. **That IN NO WAY makes YOUR ideas any less valuable.**

Nowadays, when I'm working on something I really care about, I invest in bringing in *the very best* "outside eyes" I can possibly bring in-- because **I can think of no better use of resources than enlisting the help of people who are truly exceptional at what they do.**

I see a lot of people in Facebook groups (*and mine is no exception*) giving each other advice. **People *love* to dish out free advice**. The only trouble is, *not all of that advice is good*. In fact, some of it is downright TERRIBLE!

Which is why it pays to enlist the help of *people you trust--* people who've proven to you that they know what they're doing, are doing it successfully and continue to invest in their own education so they will continue to stay on top of their game, **no matter what might change** in their respective industries.

Every time I've invested in coaching or consulting, I've seen results-- MAJOR results-- because being around high performers raises my game, *just like it's going to raise yours*, IF (and only if) you go into that sort of relationship in the right frame of mind.

Whatever you do, whomever you hire, you CANNOT get results with a "I sure hope this works for me" mentality. The ONLY WAY to get results from these sorts of investments is to fully commit that you will do whatever you need to do to MAKE IT WORK!

I got nowhere after YEARS of trying to go it alone and get all my answers for free. Once I stopped making fear-based decisions and committed to go ALL IN and invest in myself FEARLESSLY, **my business absolutely EXPLODED in a mere matter of months.**

And it wasn't because of some magical fairy dust that somebody sprinkled over my head, either-- it's because I decided with 100% certainty that if **I was going to invest at that level, then dang it, I would also commit and take responsibility at that level.**

That's why it worked for me, and it's also why it can work for you.

The reason I wanted to bring this up is because I think a lot of people hesitate to ask *(let alone pay)* others for help because we think it somehow means admitting that we're deficient in some way, that we're not good enough.

But that's just not true.

*You ARE good enough **right now.***

But you're still only one person. You only have so much space in that brilliant brain of yours, and we can ALL benefit from outside help. **There is absolutely NO shame in that.**

So if you've been feeling in your gut that you might be able to benefit from the help of someone like me (or not like me-- anybody, really!) then here's my challenge to you-- dig a little bit deeper into that feeling.

If you're hesitating because you think you can't afford it, then answer me this: what would it take to become to be the type of person who CAN afford it?

Are you confident that you'll become that person by continuing to do what you're doing, or **do you feel like you could get there more easily or more quickly by enlisting the help of someone you trust?**

Because often, *when we need help the most is when we feel the LEAST prepared to invest in it.* That was the case for me, anyway.

But now, looking back, I am CERTAIN that I would not have accomplished the things I've accomplished today if I hadn't taken that leap of faith-- **which is why I'll continue to do it, again and again, indefinitely.**

It's those moments of decision-- when you decide to bet on yourself *(not me, not anybody else, but YOURSELF)* and say, I am worth investing in.

When I make investments in ME, I get a better return on those investments than on any others I make, because money and possessions may come and go, but me?

*I'm going to be around **forever**, baby!*

Don't shortchange yourself.

Don't underestimate what you're capable of.

When you combine your superpowers with the superpowers of other awesome people, whoa...

*THAT's when you become **unstoppable.***

• •

Where Do We Go From Here?

If at this point you're super excited about using the phenomenal cosmic power of personality marketing to build an empire around your personal brand, the best thing you can do after you finish this book is to TAKE MASSIVE ACTION.

What KIND of massive action?

Hard to say-- but my hope is that working through the exercises in this book has given you some great ideas to get started on right away.

By now, you know how to **think like a media company**. You know (at least in principle) how to **set yourself apart from your competitors**. You know how to **overcome some of the most common obstacles** (both internal AND external) that might have prevented you from having success with your content marketing efforts in the past.

But after all of that, you might still be wondering:

- What about ME SPECIFICALLY will my ideal customer find aspirational?
- What about MY SPECIFIC MESSAGE and BRAND could be different from what I've heard and seen *a thousand times before* from my industry's biggest influencers?
- How do I create the EXPERIENCE of using my product or service in an automated sales funnel without losing the human touch and without giving away too much for free?
- What exactly should I SAY in my videos, ads and sales pages to get people to want to buy my stuff?
- What should I definitely NOT say?
- What SPECIFIC LEAD MAGNET should I be using as "bait" to attract my perfect customers?
- What should I be focusing on FIRST, based on the SPECIFIC STUFF I've already done and the SPECIFIC STUFF I want to do?
- Once I know what I want my ads and funnels to SAY and OFFER, how do I actually set them up so they'll WORK?

- How do I adapt to changes in the results of my ads, and/or what do I do when Facebook ads get too expensive to compete? Where do I go then, and what will I DO there? How do I protect myself NOW before that day comes?
- If stuff isn't working, how do I know WHAT TO FIX FIRST, or even HOW to FIX IT?
- When I'm ready to do the PR thing and *really* go for world domination, how do I make myself/my product seem NEWSWORTHY enough to feature?
- How do I incorporate personality marketing into a more high-touch, hands on, high ticket sales process to increase my close rates?
- ...and so on, and so on...

There are a million more questions like that that can come up as you set out to do the work of building your "media company" marketing platform.

As you might imagine, those are all questions we'd need to talk about personally to figure out.

Which is why, if it's ok with you, I'd like to take a minute or two to **walk you through what some of your possible "next steps" might be**, should you decide you'd like to get some personality marketing help from me and/or my team when you finish reading.

Remember early on when I promised to be super clear about what you could do if you wanted my support on the road to the A-List?

Well, **that time has come, my friend!**

Here's one possible example of how it might look for you to continue moving forward on this "customer journey" with me.

Let's pretend for a second that **you're SUPER PUMPED right now** and you're ready to *impact the world in a bigger way* and *start getting better results* from your content marketing efforts.

You finish the book thinking, *"Yes! That sounds awesome, I totally want that and I would LOVE some help doing it as effectively and as quickly as possible!"*

If that's the case, you pop on over to brittanybullen.com/chat, click a few buttons, answer a few questions and **your info goes straight to my inbox**. At that point, my team and I review your answers to the questions and determine that, yes, **you ARE as awesome as I suspect you are**, and would be a GREAT candidate for coaching and/or some done-for-you services to help execute on the strategy we'll build together..

We let you know as much, and you decide to move forward with a coaching relationship. *Yay!*

Assuming that's the way this goes down, here's what will happen next.

Our first (and most important!) order of business will be to zero in on three things: your *message*, your *market*, and the *method(s)* we'll use to sell your stuff.

Once we're clear on the big idea that YOU as the celebrity are going to represent, we'll identify the audience who's most likely to connect with you (*and be most likely to buy what you're offering*), because **it's not always the audience that you might think.**

I'll put my "casting director" glasses on and determine *how to channel your particular brand of "star power" into a persona that feels authentic to you,* but a persona that also is perfectly catered to who your specific audience needs you to be.

So we'll dive into your story, your experience, your passions and your personality and fuse them all together in a way that you're going to be really excited to implement.

Once we've established where we want to go, it then becomes my job to help you get there by *working with you every step of the way* to help you **say the right things at the right time** in order to give your audience the *maximum possible motivation to buy*

without being manipulative or sleazy about it.

We'll talk about videos.

We'll talk about your offers.

We'll talk about ads, emails, sales pages, order pages, even offline stuff like direct mail, if needed-- all of that lovely stuff we marketers love to design to generate those coveted leads and sales on autopilot for you!

Once we've got all of those things up and running profitably for you, we'll just grow it and optimize it from there.

We'll talk about conversion optimization.

We'll talk about scaling your ad spend.
We can even start moving into PR stuff like getting you featured on podcasts...

Maybe you can write a book...

Maybe we can work on bringing in some affiliates for you...

Whatever makes most sense for you and your business. .

Remember, I have an amazing team over at NerdyGirl.co to help facilitate all of this for you, so there's no need to be overwhelmed-- you don't have to do all of this alone.

Which is a pretty cool thing, when you think about it.

NONE OF US is in this alone.

As entrepreNERDs, we are part of a special club. We don't think like other people do. *We OBSESS.*

While other people are content to watch Netflix and scroll jealously through their news feeds watching other people do stuff, we're over here DOING STUFF.

I mean, Netflix might still be on in the background... *but we're doing stuff all the same.*

I'm honored that you allowed me into your world to geek out for a bit about the stuff that makes ME nerdy... **but now it's your turn.**

I sincerely hope that you'll find a way to put YOUR special and unique variety of nerdiness to good use in the work that you do every day. I can tell you from experience that doing business becomes a WHOLE LOT MORE FUN when you do.

And having a CRAP-ton of fun while you do the work you do?

Well, my friend, **that's the best way in the whole wide world to *sell more stuff*.**

Like This? Then You'll LOVE ....

The NerdyGirl (and Guy!) Mastermind Group on Facebook

Want to hang out with me online? The best place to find me is in my free Facebook group, the NerdyGirl (and Guy!) Mastermind. I share fun free content all the time in there, and my community is full of fun, down-to-earth entrepreNERDs just like you and me to get to know.

Come join the party at facebook.com/groups/nerdygirlmastermind today!

My "Nerd Moments" Podcast on iTunes

If you're too busy with your world domination plans to watch a lot of video content, you can take my regular marketing thought nuggets with you on the go in audio form in my podcast, Nerd Moments.

For extra efficiency, you can even listen the way I like to listen-- at 2x speed!

To find it, just search for Nerd Moments on iTunes.

Done-for-You Services by NerdyGirl.co

My original company, NerdyGirl.co, is still serving clients like you-- providing a la carte marketing services from graphic design to web design to PPC ad management and everything in between (as long as it has to do with marketing, that is)!

Visit NerdyGirl.co to get in touch with my team to find out how we can help you sell more stuff!

The EntrepreNERDfest

Want to hang out with me in person? Come join me at the nerdiest, game-changing-est, AWESOMEST three day celebration of entrepreneurship the western US has ever seen.

Get more details and secure your spot (space is limited!) at entrepreNERDfest.com.

Want to Work with Me in Some Way?

Whether you need a consultant, coach, podcast guest or speaker, you can get in touch with my team directly at nerdygirl.co/contact-us and we'll make sure your message gets where it needs to go.

I can't wait to get nerdy with you! Hope to talk to you soon,

Very Special
THANKS

to these enterprising women and men who have graciously provided us with screen captures of their video marketing!

Jessica Abito
Sara Arrington
Meagan Bender
April Bernd
Heather Brown
Kristin Calhoun
Hope Castillo
James Cauley
Lauren Cheatle Courtney
Kelly Cornelsen
Celia Coughlin-Surridge
Stephanie Danner
Johnna Dean
Janna Denton-Howes
Josephine Dunaway
Cheryl Engelhardt
Sarah Fabrizio
Paige Filliater
Jordan Gill
Veronica Greenwell
Amy Hagerup
Rebekah Hartley
Whitney Kordsiemon
Erin Kreitz Shirey
Aleksandra Laird
Katie Larson
Anna Lawrie

Erica Lewis
Linda Lopeke
Erin Lydy
Christina Maloney
Siara Martin
Samantha Maschari
Kelly Mendenhall
Tracy Moore
Marci Moore
Susan Myers-Sutton
Tanya Patxot
Tiffani Reese-Robinson
Alison Reeves
Angela Sago
Katy Simpson
Amanda Sliski
Anne Smith
Brandon Smits
Dori Spencer
Sophie Stanley
Jade Steckly
Yesenia Swecker
Dee Tchalemian
Rebekah Troyer
Dawn Wade
Terri Willingham
Samantha Wilson

A VERY NERDY MANIFESTO

Entrepreneurship is my JAM
enthusiasm is my superpower
THE PURSUIT OF AWESOMENESS
is my obsession
I refuse to be boring
While others are content to watch Netflix and
scroll jealously through their news feeds
I'm over here making stuff HAPPEN
I'M NOT A POTATO PERSON
I reject the word impossible
I fight the urge to be ordinary
I fight the urge to quit, to hide or to hesitate
and I will not rest
until I discover my own magic formula
to easily and effortlessly sell more stuff
serve more people
AND CHANGE MORE LIVES
than an ordinary human ever could
Because I'm not an ordinary human.
I AM A NERD.

Made in the USA
Monee, IL
08 September 2019